BARRY PICKTH***

"No Guts-No Glory"

The Dramatic Story of
Chay Blyth's British Steel Challenge
Yacht Race Around
The World

carfax publishing company

CARFAX PUBLISHING COMPANY

This book is dedicated to the
men and women who took
up Chay Blyth's challenge
and proved to be far from
ordinary

First published in Great Britain in
1993 by
Carfax Publishing Company,
PO Box 25, Abingdon,
Oxfordshire OX14 3UE, England.
Telephone: 0235 555335

ISBN 0902 879 308

Editor Adrian Morgan

A VIVID design and production
Design © Paul Hooper/
Mike Rubens, 172 Arlington Road,
London NW1 7HL. Telephone: 071
267 3537

The author and publisher would like
to express their thanks to British
Steel plc and to Chay Blyth's race
team without whose generous
support this remarkable story could
not have been told

Charts courtesy The Times Graphics
Dept, London

Nuclear Electric drawing copyright
© Eric North and Mark Bosanquet-
Bryant

Results BT Race Results System
Data
Copyright © British
Telecommunications plc 1992

Text paper: Enso Matt 130gsm
Cover board: Enso Gloss 300gsm
Supplied by: Enso Marketing,
New Mill Road, Orpington BR5 3QA
Tel: 0689 836911 Fax: 0689 829732

Printed and bound in Great Britain by
Burgess, Thames View, Abingdon,
Oxfordshire OX14 3LE

C O N T E N T S

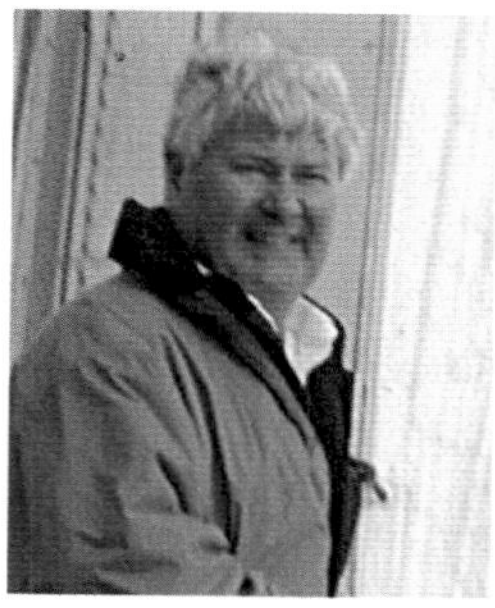

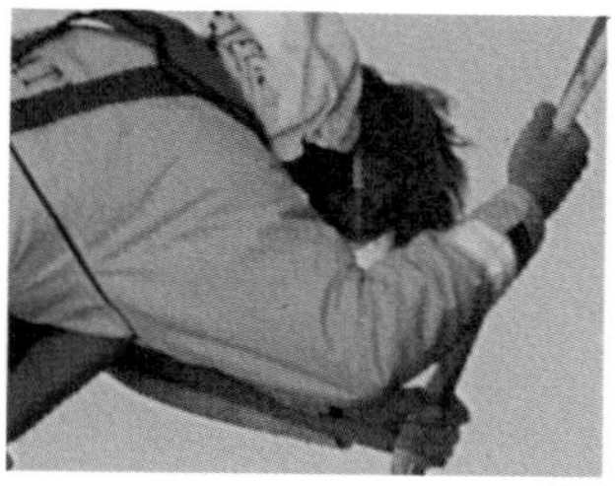

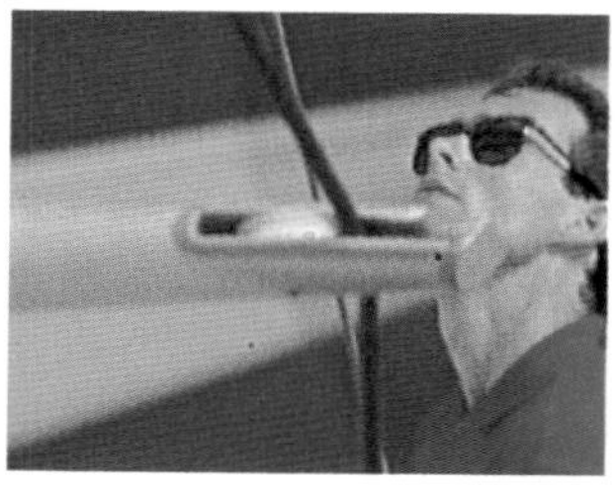

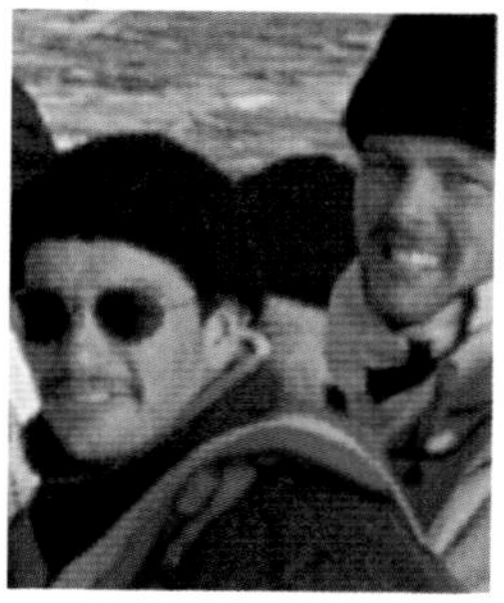

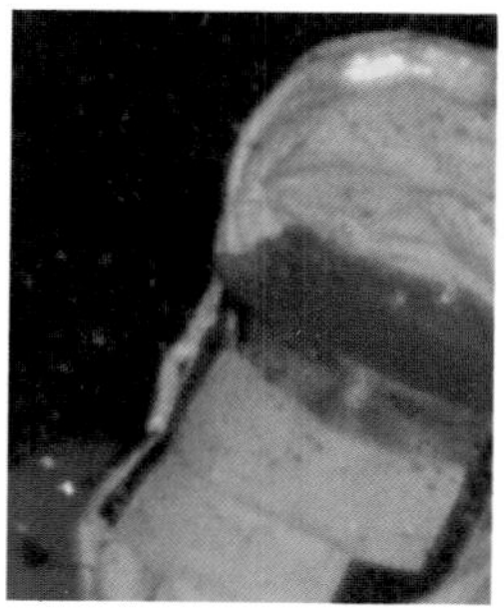

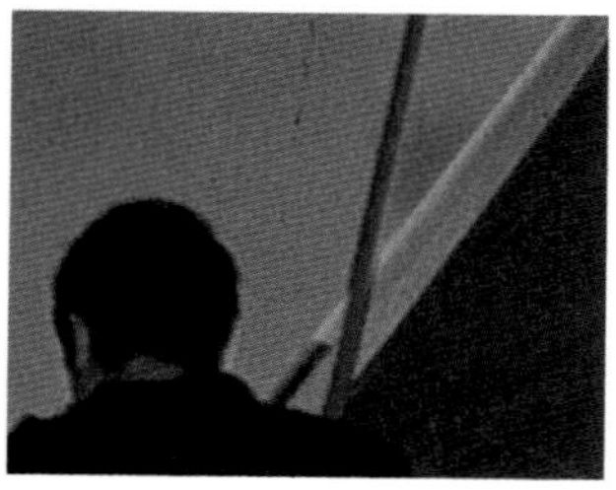

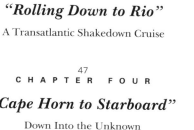

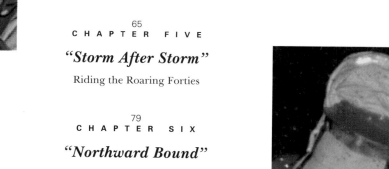

I decided I should like to take part in the British Steel Challenge on the day it was announced, the same day Tony Allen and I renamed our boat Creighton's Naturally for the last Whitbread. Needless to say Chay Blyth stole our thunder. But I never thought for a moment "if you can't beat them join them", just what a marvellous idea it was - a grander version of how we proposed to race our boat with a fare-paying crew.

I envisaged the British Steel Challenge would be a cruise-cum-race. I was wholly wrong. It didn't take much subsequent thought to realise why Chay Blyth's unusual selection process has produced, to my mind but not theirs, such extraordinary "ordinary" people.

They had seen and heard of the relentless spite of the Southern Ocean yet paid £15,000 in anticipation of being subjected to months of remorseless physical and mental strain.

It didn't stop there; a demanding training schedule, loss of earnings, expensive stopovers and family sacrifices also had to be considered. Some merely made out a cheque - these were the achievers to whom second best is not readily acceptable. Others had to use considerable effort and determination to raise what to them was a huge amount of money.

These two types were the main ingredients in the ten highly motivated and competitive crews. No wonder that my early problem was not to motivate them but to get them to back off before they reduced the boat to rubble.

At the outset, searching for some sensible reason for taking part, I said it attracted the sort of people who's company I enjoy. This has proved to be absolutely true.

Big boats are similar to ships, skills have to be assessed and used for the crews' and boat's sake. Surprises emerge as deckmen exhibit courage and determination battling knee deep in freezing water on a bucking foredeck. Astonishingly to me, they enjoy it, shun the comparative comfort of the cockpit and positively refuse to turn their active minds to number-crunching below decks.

As usual I have learned a lot. But on this race I have seen these people use fresh minds to crack some of the old chestnuts that I have never managed to solve in all my years at sea.

When I first thought about the Challenge I wondered whether Chay Blyth and his team would cope with the complicated and expensive difficulties in providing a backup at the stopovers. Each Whitbread boat has its own backup team but here was one small team dealing with ten boats raced more strenuously to windward in extreme conditions than I hitherto had thought possible.

They not only coped but managed to keep both crews and sponsors - who frequently don't have the same interests - happy. Indeed I haven't heard a murmur from any crew member that they didn't consider the £15,000 well spent.

One of the many unusual aspects of the race was the close inter-boat friendships formed during training prior to the race. Despite fierce competition amongst boats these friendships endured and the camaraderie at the stopovers was almost tangible.

I was flattered to be asked to write a foreword for Barry Pickthall, one of the few yachting journalists who didn't sit on the fence at the outset of the challenge.

Finally, there are no losers in this race. Every one of the crews can walk ten-foot tall and I am privileged to have sailed with them.

John Chittenden

John Chittenden
Skipper, Nuclear Electric

Introduction.

Shortly after noon on 26 September 1992, HRH the Princess Royal fired a cannon from the shores of the Solent which was to launch one of the greatest adventures of modern times. It was also to signal the start of an enterprise that would change forever the lives of the 182 amateur yachtsmen and women who had heeded the call of a bluff, visionary ex-soldier with nerves of steel.

One hundred and thirty of them, ranging in age from 21 to 62, lead by professional skippers, sailed

Essence of a Challenge: heavy weather in the Great Southern Ocean aboard Pride of Teesside. This is what the crews paid nearly £15,000 to experience

that memorable day from a crowded Solent aboard ten identical steel yachts on The British Steel Challenge - an eight-month, 28,000-mile voyage that would take them east-west around the world. The remainder - the "one-leggers" - would join their crew mates later at the official stopover ports of Rio de Janeiro in Brazil, Hobart in Tasmania, and Cape Town at the tip of Africa.

The event was the inspiration of one Chay Blyth, adventurer, ex-paratrooper and the first man to sail around the world alone against the prevailing winds and currents. The race was to mark the 21st anniversary of his own record-setting non-stop solo circumnavigation over the same "wrong way" route aboard the 59ft ketch British Steel in 1971.

The Challenge was quickly dubbed "the toughest yacht race ever" and attracted more than 1,000 applications. For those signing on for the whole route, the cost was almost £15,000 and it would take a year out of their lives.

Blyth's brave band of men and women came from almost every walk of life - salesmen, doctors, a vet, nurses, farmers, insurance brokers and a market gardener. Seventy per cent of them had never been sailing before they took on the challenge, and before setting off they were to undergo a rigorous training programme, logging between 3,000-5,000 sea miles, to prepare for the rigours and hardships that would lie ahead.

The yachts, built in a Devonshire shipyard, carried the sponsorship colours of ten blue-chip companies: British Steel, the Heath Insurance Group, Hofbräu Lager,

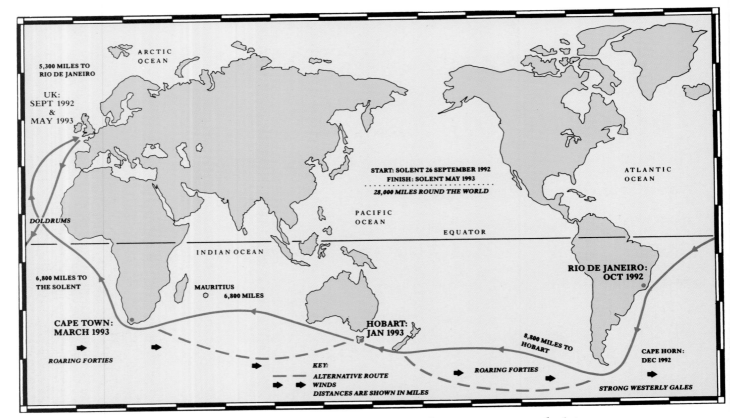

5,300 MILES TO
RIO DE JANEIRO

UK:
SEPT 1992
&
MAY 1993

ARCTIC
OCEAN

ATLANTIC
OCEAN

START: SOLENT 26 SEPTEMBER 1992
FINISH: SOLENT MAY 1993
28,000 MILES ROUND THE WORLD

DOLDRUMS

PACIFIC
OCEAN

EQUATOR

INDIAN OCEAN

6,800 MILES TO
THE SOLENT

MAURITIUS
6,800 MILES

RIO DE JANEIRO:
OCT 1992

CAPE TOWN:
MARCH 1993

HOBART:
JAN 1993

8,800 MILES TO
HOBART

CAPE HORN:
DEC 1992

ROARING FORTIES

ROARING FORTIES

KEY:
ALTERNATIVE ROUTE
WINDS
DISTANCES ARE SHOWN IN MILES

STRONG WESTERLY GALES

Rhône-Poulenc, Group 4 Securitas, Commercial Union Assurance, Nuclear Electric, International Paint, Coopers & Lybrand and The Teesside Development Corporation.

The course would trace a route down through the North-East Trades, across the Doldrums, that notorious area of frustrating calms spanning the Atlantic just north of the Equator, and on through the South-East Trades to Rio de Janeiro. In November the fleet would then thread a course through a field of icebergs off the River Plate and around Cape Horn, before straining rigs and rigging to breaking point in the brutal bash westwards across the South Pacific to Tasmania.

From Hobart the crews would resume their battle with the hostile Southern Ocean, against the might of the Roaring Forties, tracking south of Australia and across the Indian Ocean. And in mid-March they would finally reach Cape Town via the Kerguelen Islands before the homeward run

to Southampton, two months later.

Ten sturdy 67ft yachts, designed by David Thomas specifically for the Challenge, were built of steel at the DML Shipyard at Devonport. Identical one-design yachts, they would race on level terms and without handicap. Whichever crew finished back in Southampton with the shortest elapsed time for the four legs, would be the winner.

The Challenge was as simple - and as difficult - as that!

Baptism of steel at DML: differences between the yachts were too small to be measured

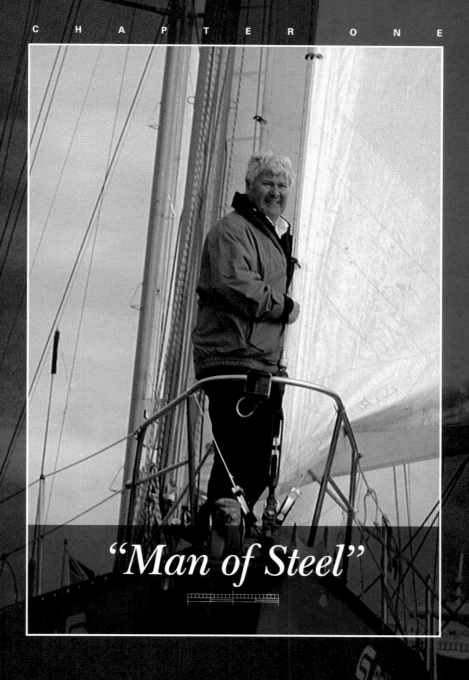

"Man of Steel"

Chay Blyth: Inspiration for a Challenge

"No guts-no glory." The paratroopers' motto that

Chay Blyth has lived by for most of his life must have been ringing in the ears of all the British Steel Challenge crews as they rounded Cape Horn and met their first Southern Ocean storm. "When things got really bad, it kept us going," admitted Adrian Rayson, aboard Heath Insured. "If one man could face that kind of weather alone we, as a crew of 14, could certainly do the same."

Blyth's pioneering solo circumnavigation in 1970/71 remained the focus and inspiration for all those who took up the Challenge. If life became uncomfortable, they had only to pick up his book "The Impossible Voyage" to find that he had endured far worse.

Ironically, as the fleet neared Tasmania, with one of the yachts dismasted and four others jury rigged to support cracked masts or broken stays, the phrase was thrown back at Blyth. He had attempted to change the course on the subsequent leg across the Indian Ocean to avoid the worst of the Roaring Forty latitudes. Over 80 per cent of these recruits voted to face the dangers head on. "We signed on for this Challenge knowing the dangers, and we didn't want it watered down half-way round," explained an indignant Rayson. Blyth's disciples had come of age.

Twenty-eight years earlier, Blyth had more than lived up to his own code when rowing from Cape Cod to Ireland with fellow paratrooper John Ridgway. "Everyone thought we were going to die - and two of our rivals did," he recalls now of that pioneering transatlantic voyage. The 3,000-mile feat took 92 days, earnt him fame and brought the clear realisation that most of us have a desire to face elements of danger at some point in our lives. "If you don't want risk or excitement, buy a bag of cotton wool and sit inside," he says dryly. It is a belief on which he has traded ever since.

One of seven children born to a Hawick railwayman, Blyth made the Army his life. And the Army made him. At the time, he was the youngest to win promotion to sergeant since the Second World War and so relished the role that he refused to climb to the commissioned ranks. The experience taught him above all that nothing is impossible. "To begin with, I knew nothing about sailing - I couldn't even navigate," recalls the

> "If you don't want risk or excitement, buy a bag of cotton wool and sit inside."

Scot. "I saw it as an adventure, with the ocean providing one of the last great challenges. I thought I would teach myself as I went along - and did - which got up the noses of the bar-room gin-and-tonic brigade, because it destroyed the cosy image that sailing is elitist and takes a lifetime to learn."

Blyth went on to win both round Britain and transatlantic races and complete three circumnavigations, two of them as a Whitbread race competitor. But he was also to taste defeat. After rowing the Atlantic, he enrolled in the Sunday Times Golden Globe challenge to become first to sail around the world non-stop alone. The incentive, perhaps, was that Ridgway, his former rowing partner had also entered. Blyth also had the offer of a free yacht.

As it turned out the yacht was to prove totally unsuitable for riding the Southern Ocean swells. Sponsorship also proved a problem. One company sent a Royal Navy officer to test him on his navigation and seamanship skills. Blyth failed. He also turned down a £12,000 offer from one newspaper because its editors wanted the boat to carry their title as its name. "That was a silly mistake - and the biggest lesson I have learned," he says with regret.

Blyth threw in the towel shortly after rounding the Cape of Good Hope. He had discovered that his bilge-keeler was almost uncontrollable when running before the Roaring Forties, and returned home to plot a fresh adventure.

So impressed was he by Robin Knox-Johnston's achievement in completing the Golden Globe within 313 days, he proposed to sail around the world the opposite way. "I was naive. I didn't realise there was any big difference between what Robin had achieved, and going round the other way against the prevailing winds and currents," Blyth admits.

British Steel was his first call on the sponsorship trail. "That was something of a coup. My approach coincided with their plans to launch a major marketing campaign," he recalls. Surprisingly, what impressed the steel men most was Blyth's

Inspiration: artist David Cobb's impression of British Steel's battle against the elements. Whenever life became too tough, Blyth would spur his yacht on with shouts of: "Come on Brit. Show me the way home."

CHAY BLYTH CBE, BEM.

Born: May 14, 1940, Hawick, Scotland. Divorced with one child, Samantha (born 1967). Awarded the BEM in 1966 and CBE in 1971 for services to yachting. Lives at Petersfield, Hampshire. 1966: with fellow Paratroop Captain John Ridgway, became the first to row the Atlantic, in an open dory. Voted BBC's Man of the Year. 1970/71: aboard the 59ft ketch British Steel, became the first to sail alone non-stop westwards around the world against the prevailing winds and currents. Voted Yachtsman of the Year. Awarded the Chichester Trophy. 1973/74: aboard the 77ft ketch Great Britain II, he and a crew of paratroopers set the fastest elapsed time in the first Whitbread round the world race. 1978: the 54ft trimaran Great Britain IV, with Rob James, won the 1978 two-man Round Britain race. 1981: sailing the 65ft trimaran Brittany Ferries GB with Rob James, won the two-man Transatlantic race in record time. 1981/2: skippered United Friendly (ex-Great Britain II) in the third Whitbread round the world race. 1984: aboard the 54ft trimaran Beefeater II with Eric Blunn, capsized off Cape Horn during a record attempt between New York and San Francisco, spending 18 hours in the water before being rescued. 1986: co-skipper of Richard Branson's Virgin Atlantic II powerboat when she won the transatlantic Blue Riband from New York to the Scilly Isles. 1989/93:conceived and organised the British Steel Challenge race around the world.

failure in the Sunday Times race. "In truth, it would have been easier to die than give up, and there are a lot of people in sailing who believe you should go on regardless. I have never taken that view. If you are not winning and something breaks, then it is better to give up than finish at the back of the fleet - or worse. They knew that if there was a crisis, the promotion was unlikely to end in my death."

Blyth left Southampton on 18 October, 1970 in the purpose-built Robert Clarke-designed 59ft ketch British Steel. Two hundred and ninety-two days later, having steered by hand for more than 20,000 miles after the yacht lost its self steering off Cape Horn, he returned to the Hamble. The headlines ran "Boat of Steel - Man of Iron" and The Times described the voyage as "The most outstanding passage ever made by one man alone". Thousands came to greet him, including the Duke of Edinburgh, Prince Charles, Princess Anne and Prime Minister Edward Heath. The gin-and-tonic sailing brigade were left to splutter into their glasses.

They had said he would never do it and, in truth, the

voyage was not without its dramas. Within a week both his running poles, used to boom out the headsails when sailing before the wind, had shattered. Off Argentina, the fierce Pampero winds bent the yacht's tiller though, thankfully, the next gust straightened it.

Shortly before rounding Cape Horn he was met by HMS Endurance, the Royal Navy Antarctic survey vessel, whose crew exchanged his mail and film for fresh bread, fruit and two bottles of Scotch. The Horn was passed at 1950 GMT on Christmas Eve. After catching less than four hour's sleep during the previous three days, fatigue and depression

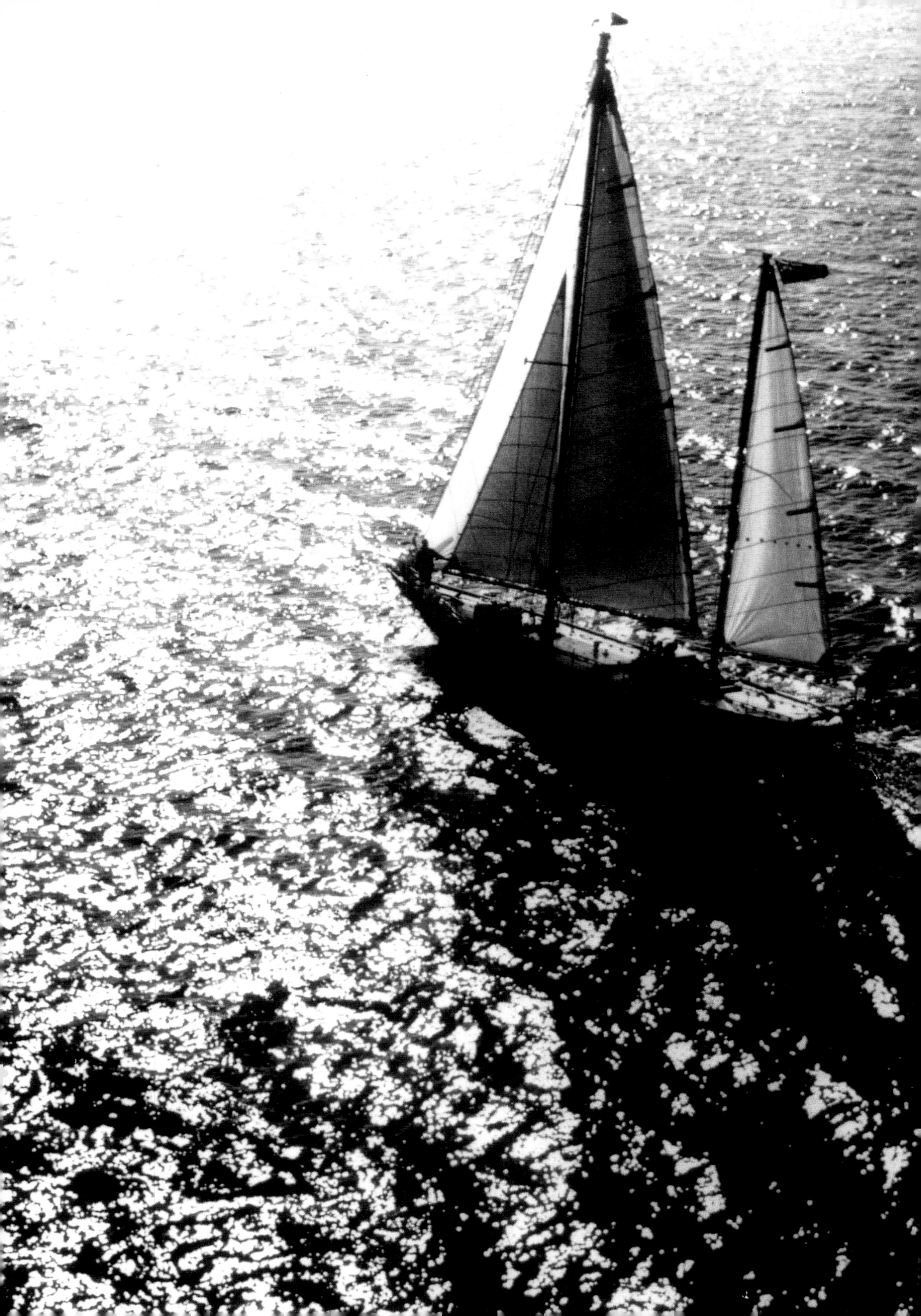

had set in. "Christmas Eve in the UK now, all the Santas filling the stockings. I feel very sad, and somehow deprived of something," he wrote in his log while thinking of his three-year-old daughter back home.

The fearful Cape: Blyth's rounding of Cape Horn marked the start of some of the most brutal weather conditions of the voyage, and 20,000 miles of hand steering

On the following day, his outlook on the world took another knock when a giant wave smashed the yacht's self steering beyond repair and hurled Blyth across the cockpit into the companionway door, leaving him with a badly gashed forehead. Faced with the prospect of steering the remaining 20,000 miles by hand, lesser men would have thrown in the towel. To rest, or shelter from the intense cold, he would now have to heave-to or lash the tiller and hope for the best.

To start with, he tried to forget about the distance and treat the voyage as a series of obstacles. When he switched to his chart of the Pacific on 28 December, he wrote in his log: "I've folded it in half so that I don't see all the sea. This way I don't think it is so far; completely nutty, but it helps."

Blyth was not the only one to think his mind had turned. Much later in the voyage, he found himself on a collision course one night with a Russian fishing vessel. When flashes from his Aldis lamp failed to draw a response, Blyth threw an explosive charge high in the air. There was a bang and a blinding flash which not only woke the man on watch, but brought the entire crew out on deck.

Once radio contact had been made, the Russian captain bottled his astonishment and asked: "Where did you leave from?"

"Southampton," came the shouted reply.

"What is your last port of call?"

"Southampton."

"Where are you going?," yelled the incredulous Russian.

"Southampton."

"How many other people on board?"

"None."

The fishermen then had their worst fears confirmed when Blyth told them of his rowing exploits across the North Atlantic!

The Southern Ocean swells continued to crash over the yacht, swamping everything in their path, including the lone yachtsman. "The waves came hissing towards me like snow-capped mountains. Sometimes the cockpit would fill and British Steel and I would be buried under great masses of foaming water. But always she would climb out again. I would just sit there like a Cheshire cat - not because I wasn't afraid, for I was often afraid, but because that's the way it's always taken me. The worse the situation gets, the funnier it seems," he wrote in his log.

He kept himself mentally alert by singing - "It surprised me just how many songs I knew" - and urging the boat on with shouts of "Come on Brit - flat out! Show me the way home".

"I would pretend to be whipping on my steed," he wrote. "It may sound silly, written down like this, but without those little games, I'd have been utterly miserable."

By the time he had sailed half way round, the boat had been flooded so many times that the smell of damp pervaded everywhere. His clothes were wet through. It was this discomfort, together with fatigue, that finally began to wear him down. "Miserable weather," he wrote. "I'm feeling tired and I'm definitely lagging. I wonder if I should increase my vitamin tablets. Half the day I'm in a trance... and moving on deck a lot without my harness. Very foolish."

But like the British Steel Challenge crews 21 years later, Blyth was to face the worst of the weather once he had passed Tasmania. In one incident, he was almost washed overboard and in another, trapped below decks when the hatches became jammed.

When not battling to keep his yacht on a steady course or bailing, he was either stitching torn sails or catching halyards before they chafed through. "There is a particular quality of venom in the seas. A viciousness not experienced even in the lonely wastes south of Cape Horn. Alone in a fierce sea you feel the ocean is making a determined effort to get you," he noted.

"Half the day I'm in a trance... and moving on deck a lot without my harness. Very foolish."

Together again: Blyth takes the helm of his old warhorse in the Solent after she was found abandoned and then restored to her former glory as an Army training yacht

Man of the moment: Blyth at the wrong end of a ducking at the hands of the 29 women who followed his call

run down by the Russian fishing vessel off Port Elizabeth, and it thrilled him. A helicopter took off and flew round him taking photographs, and as the carrier passed by, her crew lined the decks. "I felt very humble. I dipped the ensign in salute, which was rather a tricky business, as it meant leaving the tiller," Blyth wrote in his log.

He would have finished back at the Hamble three days earlier than the 292 it took to complete the voyage, had he not been asked to slow down and time his arrival to coincide with the end of Cowes Week, for what turned into a hero's welcome.

The feat certainly equalled, if not bettered, anything Francis Chichester, Robin Knox-Johnston and Alec Rose had achieved. Before the British Steel Challenge, it was a feat that only two other crews had managed to equal - David Scott Cowper who completed the same voyage in 221 days aboard his 41ft yacht Ocean Bound in 1982, and John Ridgway and Andy Briggs who sailed the 52ft ketch English Rose VI round in 193 days.

This, and the salt sores, rope burns, chilblains and rashes that ravaged his body, left Blyth bruised and humbled by the never-ending battle. "To atheists I say 'Go sailing singlehanded for a few weeks.' No one will ever say to me there is no God without my remembering all these situations."

Off Cape Agulhas, on the South African coast, the storms actually knocked his yacht back 100 miles and one wave broke right over the boat. "I just sat holding the tiller and steering under water, as if on a submarine. Apart from the mast and rigging, we were completely submerged." As the conditions warmed in the Atlantic, he took to sleeping next to the tiller in the cockpit, and re-crossed his outward track on 22 June after 247 days at sea.

"There is a particular quality of venom in the seas. A viciousness not experienced even in the lonely wastes south of Cape Horn."

Shortly afterwards, he was to have a surprise rendezvous with the British aircraft carrier HMS Ark Royal. He had just switched on the radio in readiness for a scheduled call to Portishead Radio near Bristol, when the speaker blasted out "British Steel...British Steel. This is Ark Royal."

A surprised Blyth asked if they had picked him up on radar. "If you look astern, you will see us," came the reply as Ark Royal's monster bows bore down on him. It was the first close contact with the outside world since Blyth had almost been

"Toughest Race Ever"

The Men, the Women,
the Yachts;
the Ultimate Adventure

For most of us, this story began shortly after 10pm on 3 January, 1989. That was the night ITN's News at Ten programme carried a brief item on Chay Blyth's proposed adventure race around the world. Those who missed it picked the story up in the newspapers the following morning. The Times carried a half-page feature and reported tongue-in-cheek that, while Blyth was looking for 120 adventurous men and women to sail against the prevailing winds and currents, the man who pioneered the course against the spin of the globe would this time be leading from ashore.

Readers didn't care a jot. Within hours The Times' switchboard had been overrun with callers demanding to know how to sign up. It was as if a Pied Piper's call had been broadcast into homes and offices the length and breadth of the land.

One woman rang directory enquiries and insisted on having Blyth's number. "No, I don't know his address, but there is only one Chay Blyth," she intoned. Bill Vincent, a carpenter from Bath, simply climbed into his car and headed for London to sign up there and then. To his surprise, he discovered that the former paratrooper who had caused the stir was not based at British Steel's Embankment headquarters at all. Undaunted, he caught his man at the London Boat Show and signed on before the chance was lost.

Simon Clarke, a 28-year-old director of a ski tour company, was reading about parachuting onto glaciers in Sir Ranulph Fiennes' autobiography "Living Dangerously" when the News at Ten report flashed onto the small screen. "I suddenly found myself thinking: 'If this guy can do that - something completely different and wacky - I can do the Challenge.' It gripped my imagination."

Within a week, Britain's best known yachtsman had received 150 applications. Within a month, the number had risen to 350. By the end of 1989, Blyth had turned away more than 1,000 applicants, all prepared to invest the best part of £15,000 and a year of their lives in this chance to escape from the daily grind.

"No, I don't know his address, but there is only one Chay Blyth."

More than 70 per cent of Blyth's final choice of recruits had done nothing more seamanlike than step on a cross-Channel ferry. Very few had any deep-sea sailing experience, and only a handful had raced before. "We are going to teach them to sail," Blyth told a group of sceptical yachting scribes at the launch. Most went back to their offices convinced there would be few takers, and even

fewer coming home at the end of the voyage.

The men at British Steel got it wrong too. They had insisted on a let-out clause in their contract with Blyth if less than 25 per cent of the places had been taken up nine months before the race's start on September 26 1992. The supporting sponsorship, they believed, would be much easier to secure.

In fact, the situation proved the exact opposite, for the "Pied-Piper of yachting" had his followers within weeks but did not secure the last name for his ten-strong fleet until four

The prototype training yacht British Steel Challenge gave the crews a foretaste of the race

months before the start.

The Challenge attracted men and women from almost every walk of life. There was a lorry driver, a vet, undertaker and salesman sharing the experience - if not the same night watches - with doctors, a market gardener, several insurance brokers and a prison officer. There was even an ex-convict within the group.

Between signing up and the start, most endured an intense training programme, logging between 3,000 and 5,000 miles, and more than 20 took it all so seriously that they devoted extra time to earning their Ocean Yacht Master tickets.

By the end, or rather the beginning of the end, each knew exactly what to expect in this race around the world. Training trips out into the Atlantic in mid-winter, sleep deprivation during non-stop weekend courses and delivery trips around the country gave them all a good insight into what life would be like breasting icy Southern Ocean swells in the Roaring Forties and living in a steel box without the benefits of air conditioning in the intense heat and humidity of the Tropics.

Remarkably, only 27 of Blyth's original pick threw in the towel before the start, and only one found it all too much to endure, once the race had commenced.

"They certainly knew what to expect," recalls Pete Goss, the former Green Beret responsible for turning this disparate bunch into blue water sailors. "When they first joined for training, most were starry-eyed enough just to want to sail round the world. But the training programme Chay and I put together soon knocked that out of them. After enduring months of cold night watches, wet clothes, fitness runs and 6am swims - even in mid-winter, their one wish, it seemed, was to win."

"In the early days, many clambered aboard in trepidation. Some even had to be shown how to climb up without falling over the lifelines," Goss said on the eve of the start. "Now they are happy and agile enough to work 87ft up a wildly gyrating mast while the yacht is bashing into the seas. What has motivated them is the Challenge itself. For some it has been a very steep learning curve, but through sheer tenacity and some tears, each has become a responsible seaman."

For many, just raising the money to compete in the race, was challenging enough. Some sold every asset from business to home, the fog lamps off their car to the vehicles themselves. A few even went to the extreme of making sponsored bungee jumps and sky dives. Employees of British Steel who won a place on board for one leg had to raise a minimum of £2,000 for Save The Children, the official race charity, to prove their commitment.

Among those to sacrifice much of their existing lives was Valerie Elliot, a teacher and grandmother who gave up a marriage and much else. By the time the race started, her grip-bag slung aboard Rhône-Poulenc, represented everything she owned.

Roger Pratt, a 46-year-old crewman on Hofbräu Lager, not only sold his share in an advertising agency, but his car and flat had to go too. Lisa Marie Wood, a former Wren invalided out of the Navy after sustaining severe burns in a fire, was earning little more than £6,000 as a nurse in an old peoples' home when the Challenge came up.

So determined was she to take part that her fund-raising

Hofbräu Lager: she was skippered by Pete Goss, a tough Green Beret, employed by Blyth as one of the training team to toughen up the crews prior to the race

Building up stamina and fitness for the challenge of a lifetime. Training days began with a dawn run and swim before breakfast – whatever the weather. Some crews lost as much as three stone, training weekends and holidays for 18 months in weather that ranged from flat calm to force 12. Only 27 of the original recruits threw in the towel

Assault course: some crews covered 5,000 miles in training for the race

exploits, which included selling her car bit by bit to pay for training, made her something of a legend. She got the rest of the money by writing begging letters to more than 200 companies.

Stuart Smith-Warren and Keith Snell, both British Steel employees from Gwent, raised more than £5,400 for Save The Children by organising a dinghy race. Neil Skinner from Wiltshire, Mark Lodge from Essex and Nicola Handley from Lancashire each put their hearts in their mouths and leapt out of aeroplanes for the same charity and prayed that their parachutes would open, while Louise Broadbent from Yorkshire took on the terrors of a bungee jump.

The most successful fund raiser, however, was Patrick Quinn from Manchester. He called on a publishing colleague to match his own stake. He did, giving a cheque for £15,000 to hand across to Save The Children.

The luckiest must have been Richard Scott, a 37-year-old married man with three children, who raced on InterSpray. He had been working at a British Coal pit in Durham and was one of the first recruits to the Challenge. He too was looking for sponsorship and Blyth prompted Sir Bob Scholey, then British Steel's chairman, to use his links with the Coal Board to ask them for support.

That overture failed and, three months after Scott had signed up for the race, he suffered the double blow of being made redundant. Fortunately he later found work at a Courtaulds' plant in Grimsby, but did not dare to mention plans for taking an eight-month break until a few days after his arrival. The response from his manager was blunt. "If I had known you were doing this, I would never have ****** taken you on. And NO. The company will not sponsor you" was how Scott reported the one-way conversation.

But unknown to Scott, or his manager for that matter, another meeting was to take place that same week between Sipko Huismans, Courtaulds' chief executive, and Blyth. The race chairman was winning over the Dutchman to sponsor one of the yachts, and dropped Scott's involvement into their conversation.

Corporate wheels began to whir. Within a day, an incredulous manager was informing an equally surprised Scott that he was booked on the next flight to Southampton for a dinner date with the company's managing director.

Two days later, the Courtaulds' pair joined Blyth aboard the training yacht British Steel Challenge for a corporate day's sailing around the Isle of Wight. Huismans, informed by a journalist that Scott would be losing his job, came up with an offer not just to sponsor him for the voyage, but keep him on the payroll too!

We know that Scott was gobsmacked by the offer, but the response from his manager back in Grimsby can only be imagined.

Some of Blyth's recruits were picked knowing they would have tough personal challenges to conquer first. Donald Deakin, a middle-aged company director aboard Group 4 Securitas, for instance, had to come to terms with a lifetime of corporate hospitality. He was so rotund that when pulling on a rope one day, he slipped and rolled like a ball across the deck. "At the time we all laughed, but for Don, it was a real problem," admitted Goss. "His nightmare was that he might not complete the three-mile compulsory run we set for each volunteer, and it drove him to lose three stone. By the time of the start, he was as agile as the rest."

Valerie Elliot had to conquer a fear of heights. "Going up the mast was her personal Everest," recalled Ian MacGillivray, who shared the training with Goss and later went on to skipper Pride of Teesside. "She tried several times and failed. Then, one day we had a problem at the masthead and I said 'Quick Valerie, grab the harness.' She was half way up the mast before she really knew what was happening. I went up with her, asking 'Are you OK?' but all I got were little moans in response. She got to the top, did the job - and by the time she had been lowered back on deck, she was standing 10ft tall. It was a real turning point in her life, giving her confidence a tremendous boost. She could tackle any job on board after that."

Another to overcome a serious problem, this one self-inflicted, was David Arthur, a 46-year-old director of a financial brokerage. He broke his leg and ankle during an impromptu football match against the rival crew from Rhône-Poulenc and was told that he might not make the start. Thankfully, the care from staff at Stoke Mandeville Hospital, coupled with his own iron will, got him back on British Steel II just in time for the race start.

Some fell by the wayside during the early stages of training after failing to overcome their sea sickness. Any who have endured a rough Channel crossing know that one symptom is a willingness to die, and the only cure is sitting under a tree. One afflicted recruit actually thought he was about to depart this life when his outpouring suddenly turned fluorescent green during a night watch in the Channel. Later, as the others consoled him, they were relieved to discover the reason for this supernatural outburst. He had been ill over the starboard navigation light.

During the race almost everyone got their sea legs within a day or two of the start, but one unfortunate, a one-legger who surprisingly perhaps did not suffer too badly during training, was ill for 56 days during the second stage around Cape Horn. He lost 24lbs in weight, but thankfully perked up the moment he stepped ashore at Hobart, and swore he would never go to sea again.

> "If I had known you were doing this, I would never have ****** taken you on."

Each crew member also had to master at least one skill during their training. These included everything from sail making and rigging to engineering and maintenance of essential equipment like the engine, electrical equipment and watermaker. Brian Lister, a 54-year-old insurance broker on Hofbräu Lager, was somehow given the role of cook. According to crew mates who had to endure his first offerings, he had never cooked a meal in his life. But he threw himself into the task and, after attending a cookery course at McDougalls, suppliers of the special freeze-dried food for the race, became adept at turning even the blandest fare into something special. "He and Pippa Welch, a computer programmer, shared the job of purser," said Goss. "Between them, they had to come up with a variety of menus to feed 14 people in rough weather, compromising between personal tastes, variety and the limitations we had of water and gas - and they became very good at it."

Sailing lessons began with a correspondence course, drawn up by Blyth and Goss, to provide a basic grounding while the training yacht was being built. It proved a good starter, but also led to one or two classic misunderstandings.

Roy Meakin, a 24-year-old lifeguard on Nuclear Electric, who was to turn into a very competent crewman, learned to tie every knot in his living room and name each part of the boat from the manual. But he never mastered the concept of the wind strengths which each sail could be expected to handle without blowing apart until it was explained to him later. "When he first joined us, Roy thought that if you wanted to travel at 30 knots, you merely had to set the No 2 yankee," chuckled MacGillivray.

That, and many other gaps of knowledge, was all swept away in the first round of introductory voyages. "These were long 'get-to-know-each-other' sails across the Channel to put the basics into practice and introduce everyone to sailing at night," recalls Goss. They were followed by a series of winter trips. "These were much tougher, designed not just to teach them about the boat, but the reality of life at sea. Each weekend, we covered 450 miles, often within a 14-mile radius of Plymouth. It was just one continuous round of changing sails in conditions that varied from flat calms to force 12 storms and wind-chill factors down to -30C. It shook them up - And they loved it!"

Then came the assessment sails. "We taught them how to make the boat go fast, about watch systems,

> *"It was just one continuous round of changing sails in conditions that varied from flat calms to force 12 storms and wind-chill."*

Wet work: foredeck crews took the brunt of the elements, but learnt to overcome constant drenching and freezing spray. For many the training period came as a rude awakening to the life of an ocean racing yachtsman. By the end of the training period the recruits had put more miles under their belts than most weekend yachtsmen

Over 70 per cent of the crews had never sailed before volunteering for the race

Blyth and his team of professionals had tried to cover every eventuality, training the crews to a level much higher than many Whitbread race teams in the past. But were they ready?

There were doubters.

Many professionals predicted disaster, mass disillusionment, and even death. One journalist, Stuart Alexander from the Independent newspaper, joined Rhône-Poulenc for the Fastnet race as a prelude to sailing with the crew on the stage round Cape Horn. He had the temerity to question the ability of some crew members. His article, published three days before the start, so infuriated Blyth that he gave the journalist a controversial ducking.

Alexander had written: "To Blyth, it is a simple matter of determined people being allowed to test themselves against the most difficult circumstances in the clear knowledge that they could come to grief. They know that, but whether they really believe it is another matter. A skipper could well have to decide between the safety of the boat and the rest of his charges, and saving someone who has fallen overboard."

"Reasonable but not exhaustive attempts have been made to see that the crews have been trained, but there can be nothing to prepare them for the truly wild weather they may have to face. After the only major rehearsal the BSC crews have done, 850 miles around Ushant and the Fastnet Rock, many thought they had been through the gates of hell and survived. The worst leg lasted about 35 hours in a true wind speed of 18 to 25 knots and it took only a few of those hours for many to find that it was debilitatingly unpleasant."

Many people agreed that these were fair comments, and this concern for safety, particularly for those who had not set foot on a yacht before signing up for the Challenge, had already prompted the Royal Ocean Racing Club, (RORC), Britain's premier offshore race organisation, to call Blyth in for questioning.

The three-time circumnavigator pre-empted the committee's probing with a pertinent question of his own.

"What experience do you think one needs to sail around the world?," he asked.

Blyth then relieved the pregnant silence with a suggested answer: "Not a lot. There's nothing magic about sailing. It's only wind and water, even at Cape Horn. There is danger and there will undoubtedly be problems. But these crews have all trained hard and learned how to cope with these eventualities. Everyone knows exactly what they are letting themselves in for and no one is forcing them to do it. "

"As for training, most have completed more than 3,000 hard miles. They are in far better shape than many so-called professional competitors in past Whitbread races."

It was all good uncompromising stuff, and it left Britain's senior sailors in no doubt that bases

Training took place in all weathers, day and night

had been covered. Alan Green, perhaps the greatest supporter of the race within the RORC, was particularly impressed by the commitment shown by the recruits. "We are now very pleased with the preparations," he said on the eve of the race start.

man-overboard routines and navigation, and each had to pass an exam at the end of it. There wasn't time to relax. We drove them so hard, one fellow fell asleep where he stood midway through a briefing," Goss remembers.

Blyth and his sailing masters followed this with two weekends of racing tuition in the Solent aboard a fleet of Sigma yachts. Individuals were also sent on courses to learn about cooking, first aid, sail making, maintenance and photography. Then, nine months before the start, the list of recruits was broken down into ten equal teams, taking into account age, strengths and abilities. To ensure fair play, the sponsors were then called on to pull their team out of a hat.

From that point on it was up to each professional skipper to meld his or her crew into a winning team. They took very different approaches. Alec Honey, the initial choice of skipper aboard Rhône-Poulenc, took his charges to live for a week in total isolation at a house in Brittany. The French sponsor later commissioned Whitbread race winner Lionel Pean to coach them, and also brought in a sports psychologist to monitor their progress.

Other sponsors called on experienced names like the five-times Whitbread veteran Peter Blake to give pep talks or lessons on the finer points of sail setting and yacht racing.

In August, six weeks before the start of the race, crews had the chance to put all this into practice during a race from Southampton to the Fastnet Rock and back. During the 850-mile slog they experienced the full gamut of conditions, and each team had to practice man-overboard routines and cope with medical difficulties, including having their skippers confined to their bunks for 24 hours.

"These people have covered more miles than many weekend yachtsmen will do in a lifetime."

John Chittenden, a former cruising secretary of the Royal Yachting Association (RYA) who had also skippered the racer/cruiser Creighton's Naturally in the previous Whitbread race, said of his charges aboard Nuclear Electric: "Safety has been paramount throughout the training. We have practiced man-overboard routines and getting into liferafts as well as racing in heavy weather."

Behind the criticisms from these old salts was the sub-conscious belief perhaps that this race could destroy the exclusive aura and mystique that surrounds much of yachting. After all, if a farmer with no previous sailing experience can race around the world, what is so special about yacht racing in the Solent or English Channel?

"The best part about having people who had not sailed before was the fact that they had not picked up any bad habits," said Goss. "As a result, the wearing of harnesses - and clipping on - is now second nature to them, just as children put seat belts on the moment they get in a car. If professional sailors did the same, fewer would have been lost in past Whitbread races."

By the time they had reached Cape Town at the end of the toughest stage through the Southern Ocean, a large number would be particularly thankful for those harnesses - and the safety routines that Goss and MacGillivray had drummed into them.

The race was to be a unique adventure for amateurs, but the concept of paying crews and inexpensive one-design yachts also offered sponsors a unique opportunity to get involved at a fraction of the cost of running a Whitbread yacht. To Blyth the event was based on a very simple

Interspray: Paul Jeffes and his crew power back from their "training" Fastnet

philosophy. "We are not into sailing. We are into the sailing business. Whether it be a crew member or sponsor, we are offering each a set package for a set price. They know exactly what they are getting and there are no additions."

It was this direct approach that attracted marketing men like Duncan Hall, the chief executive of the Teesside Development Corporation to stump up the better part of £225,000 to have one of the ten yachts racing under their colours. "This race appealed to me on three counts," explained this straight-talking northerner. First, I can relate to the crews. There is no mystique, even for a non-yachtie like myself. Secondly, all the yachts are identical so we stand an equal chance of winning. Finally, the race is part of a package that has involved corporate hospitality, provided us with a great many publicity

opportunities, and win or lose, will keep Teesside in the news."

Hall was so impressed with the package that he took almost no time to decide, surprising Blyth by cutting him off five minutes into a well-rehearsed presentation. "It's OK Chay, we are going to do it. We're sold on it. Now let's talk about details."

If only all the presentations had gone that easily. In truth, if Blyth could have foreseen the depths to which the recession would hit British industry he would have probably put the race off for five years - or not done it at all. But having taken the plunge in 1989 and won over British Steel as the title sponsor, there was no turning back. He tackled the formidable task of raising the best part of £4 million with a degree of verve and enthusiasm that is all too rare. While so many were talking themselves down in the recession, he and his marketing man, Michael Kay, were banging on doors, drums and whatever else came to hand, to sell the concept.

He began by working down the list of principal suppliers to British Steel, but his approaches were not always conventional. First port of call was the Heath Insurance Group. As brokers for much of British Steel's insurance business, the company had insured the Scotsman's original British Steel yacht. Talking over lunch the directors found his proposals interesting but wondered why an insurance broker would want to sponsor a race yacht. "Because you could lose British Steel's business, if you don't," Blyth answered with a twinkle in his eye.

Heath in turn drew Commercial Union into the Challenge and had a bet on the side that their yacht would beat CU back to Southampton. The Group was also responsible, in an oblique way, for Group 4 Securitas signing up for a yacht. John MacKensie-Green, the chief executive at Heath, invited some of their top clients, including Jorgen Philip-Sorensen, the chairman of Group 4, for a day of corporate sailing in the Solent during Cowes Week.

"It was an unforgettable day" recalls MacKensie-Green. "After leaving Ocean Village, we passed the QE2 in Southampton Water, were buzzed by the Red Arrows in the Solent, and later sailed alongside Lawrie Smith's Whitbread yacht Rothmans." Sorensen was clearly taken by the idea of the Challenge, but what sealed Group 4's involvement was the sight of another yacht bearing the name of the rival security firm, Securicor. "OK. We'll have one," he said. Only at the end of the

The fleet gathered at St Katharine Dock, in London, where corporate sponsors were given ample opportunity to scrutinise their eight-month investment and meet some of the crews. This aspect of Blyth's plan was crucial to the Challenge's success

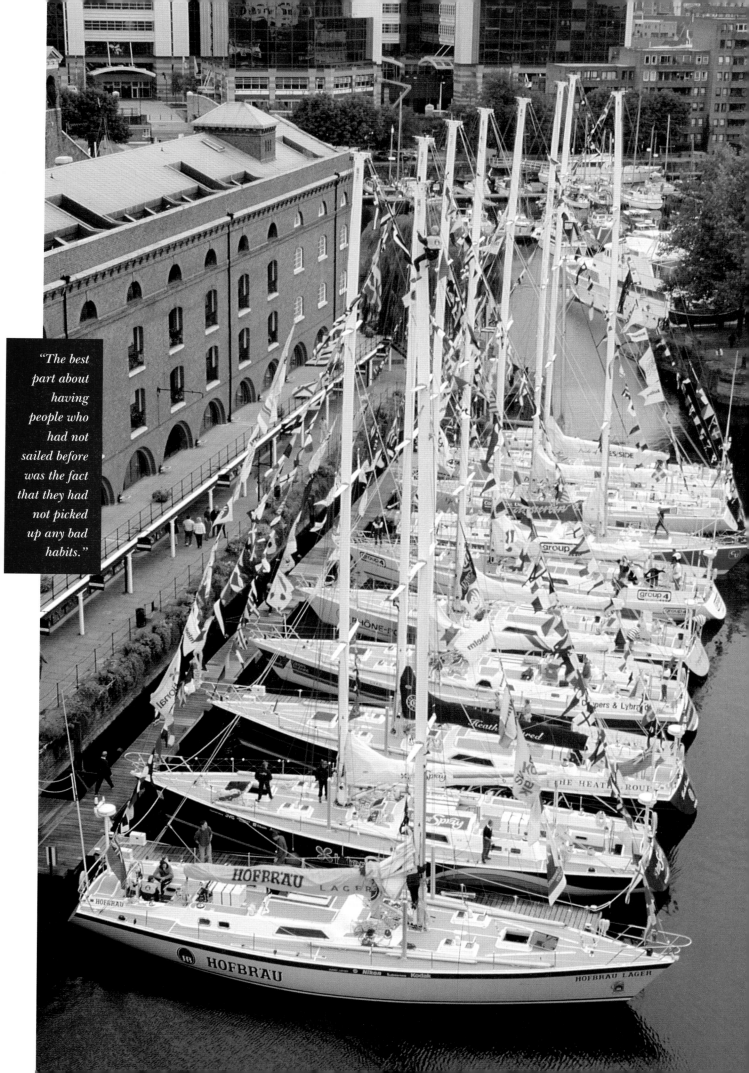

"The best part about having people who had not sailed before was the fact that they had not picked up any bad habits."

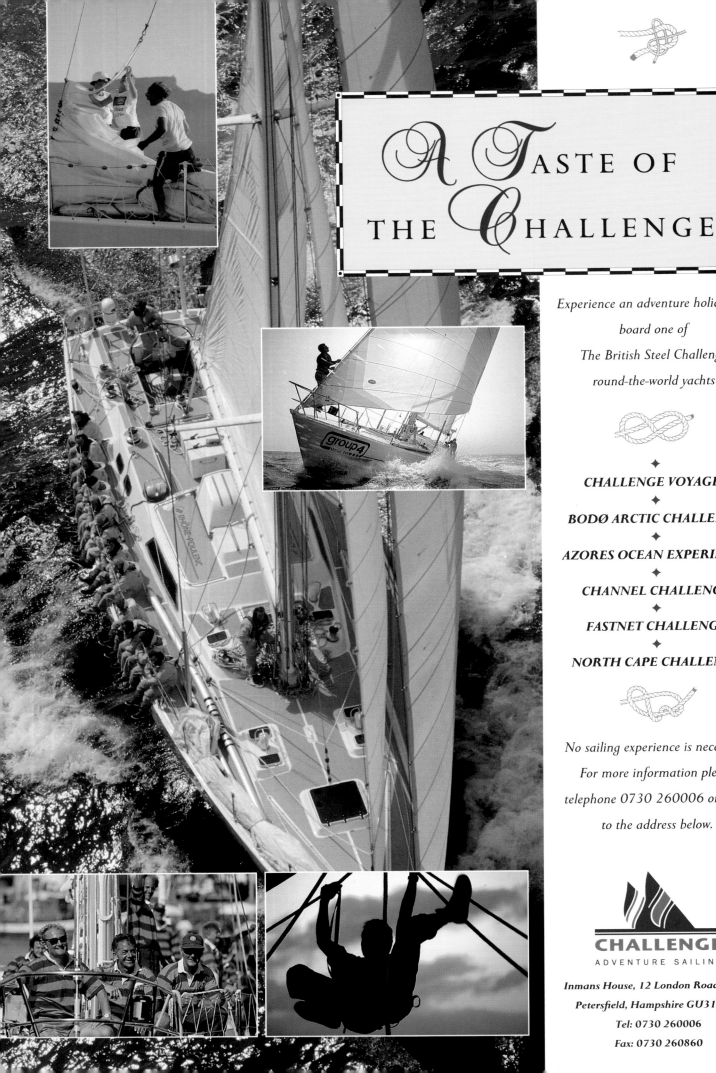

A Taste of the Challenge

day, did the Group 4 boss ask the cost of it all.

Rhône-Poulenc provide British Steel with more than £3 million of pickling chemicals, and being French owned its management was well attuned to the benefits sailing promotions can provide. As a result, the cost of their entry was split three ways between their French, British and corporate divisions.

Coopers & Lybrand, the international accountancy group, and Nuclear Electric, also have close commercial links with British Steel. Courtaulds, on the other hand, found the race a lucrative introduction for International, their paints division. They not only provided the paint for the ten Challenge yachts, but were given the chance to quote and win a contract to supply paint for three ore carriers then under con- struction in Japan for British Steel.

Hall and Woodhouse, the Dorset-based specialist real-ale brewery used their boat to launch the Hofbräu Munich lager to pubs and off-licences across south- ern England.

On a lower scale, more than 80 companies like Nikon, IBM, Dickinson Stationery, Carfax Publishing Company and Kodak tested these uncharted sponsorship waters by paying up to £16,000 to have their name on the sides of one yacht. By all accounts, it was a great success, for they received much more than mere signage for their money. Each company also had the use of the yacht for corporate hospitality and monthly lunches held at the Royal Ocean Racing Club helped foster tremendous synergy within the group.

One tentative sponsor was overheard to brag: "I've been to three of these lunches and struck a deal at each one of them - yet haven't even signed up for the race yet."

"It turned into a club, and we are all doing new business with each other. Those introductions alone covered our sponsorship costs," said Tony Eatough whose company, Kodak, supplied all the film for the race.

What impressed Duncan Spence, head of the Carfax Publishing Company which supported Rhône-Poulenc, was the team-building aspect of the Challenge. "We used the corporate sailing days as an incentive for our staff in the hope it would help in our own team-building efforts. As the race unfolded, it became a centre point of discussion in the office, and with the aid of posters and calendars also turned into a very successful promotional vehicle for selling our academic journals around the world."

The ten identical budget racers were designed around Blyth's three "S" principals - strength, safety and simplicity. Since this one-design fleet raced alone, never competing against other designs, steel replaced more expensive construction materials like carbon fibre, and Dacron was substituted for the more exotic Kevlar and Mylar plastic film materials in the sail wardrobe. And with crews paying their way - another first - the sponsorship packages could be pitched at prices that companies could swallow whole.

The entire cost of the race came to little more than £11 million. Compare that with the £5 million budget of one maxi yacht to win the Whitbread Round the World race, and the cost represented remarkable value.

For Hall and his men selling Teesside, their boat was a bargain-basement promotion. Not only did it carry the flag around the world, providing a foot in the door to talk with foreign industrialists about in- vestment in this promising area of the North East, but it acted as a catalyst to put pride and hope back into a local population hard hit by the recession.

"Sailing is a fast, exciting spectacle," Duncan Hall explained. "There is a degree of elitism within this sport, but I am not afraid of that. What we have to do is bridge the gap just as Brian Clough has between the boxed stands and terraces at Nottingham Forest. We used this sponsorship not only to encourage new industry to the area, but to offer the unemployed of Hartlepool and Teesside the chance to have a go themselves. The aim has been to raise the profile of the sport in our area and ensure that no one can say that they never had the chance to try it."

Long before the race ended, the ethos behind the Challenge had transcended yachting circles and found strong appeal among the public at large. Everyone, it seemed, knew of someone taking part in the race, or had a child following the event as part of their school curriculum. And if they didn't, then it was sheer escapism that led up to 4,000 to call up the BT fax database each week to get the latest news and positions when the yachts were at sea, over 110,000 over the course of the race.

> *"I've been to three of these lunches and struck a deal at each one of them - yet haven't even signed up for the race yet."*

The finished article: Heath Insured and a fully trained crew

Profile of a Winner

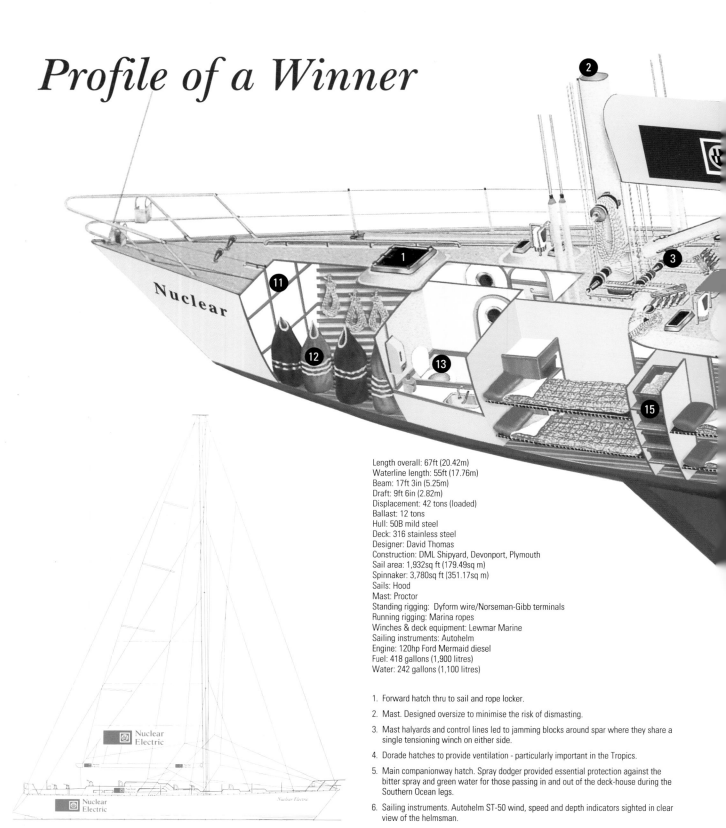

Length overall: 67ft (20.42m)
Waterline length: 55ft (17.76m)
Beam: 17ft 3in (5.25m)
Draft: 9ft 6in (2.82m)
Displacement: 42 tons (loaded)
Ballast: 12 tons
Hull: 50B mild steel
Deck: 316 stainless steel
Designer: David Thomas
Construction: DML Shipyard, Devonport, Plymouth
Sail area: 1,932sq ft (179.49sq m)
Spinnaker: 3,780sq ft (351.17sq m)
Sails: Hood
Mast: Proctor
Standing rigging: Dyform wire/Norseman-Gibb terminals
Running rigging: Marina ropes
Winches & deck equipment: Lewmar Marine
Sailing instruments: Autohelm
Engine: 120hp Ford Mermaid diesel
Fuel: 418 gallons (1,900 litres)
Water: 242 gallons (1,100 litres)

1. Forward hatch thru to sail and rope locker.

2. Mast. Designed oversize to minimise the risk of dismasting.

3. Mast halyards and control lines led to jamming blocks around spar where they share a single tensioning winch on either side.

4. Dorade hatches to provide ventilation - particularly important in the Tropics.

5. Main companionway hatch. Spray dodger provided essential protection against the bitter spray and green water for those passing in and out of the deck-house during the Southern Ocean legs.

6. Sailing instruments. Autohelm ST-50 wind, speed and depth indicators sighted in clear view of the helmsman.

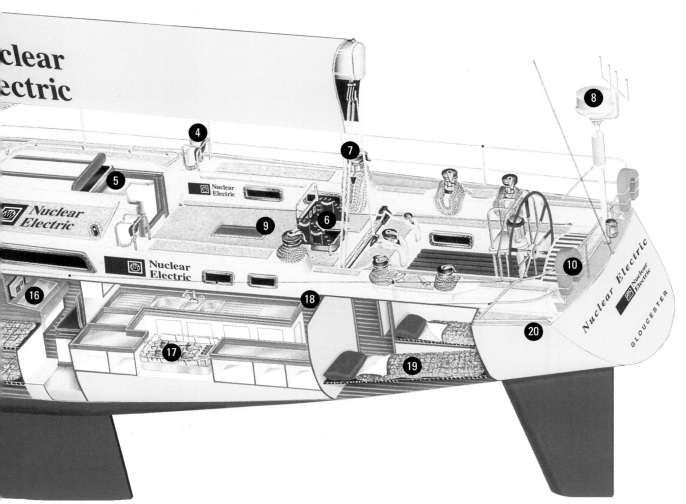

7. Winches. The deck and sail plan of these yachts was designed around the largest hand-operated self-tailing winch within the Lewmar range. Hence the limited sail area which made the yachts safe and easier to handle than an out-and-out racer.

8. Antenna and radar pole. Raytheon radar was fitted as a safety measure to help crews spot shipping in bad weather or at night as well as warn against the larger icebergs encountered in the Southern Ocean. Also mounted on the pole was the GPS navigation receiving aerial and BT's SAT-C satellite tracking and telex transmission antenna.

9. Liferafts (not shown). Two 8-person and one 6-person RFD liferafts stowed in central cockpit container ready for instant deployment, along with survival rations and equipment.

10. Man-overboard equipment. Two horse-shoe lifebuoys, each attached to a danbuoy, drogue, dye-marker and shark repellent stowed in cockpit coaming ready for instant deployment. Each crew member was also equipped with a personal EPIRB (Emergency Position Indicating Radio Beacon) fitted in a special pouch in their oilskins as well as flares to help the yacht locate them.

11. Watertight compartment. Collision bulkhead fitted 8ft from bows to provide vital protection for the crew and maintain watertight integrity in the event of a collision with an iceberg or other vessel.

12. Sail locker. Each yacht was equipped with ten sails for the race and crews received a penalty for those lost or damaged beyond repair.

13. Heads. Toilet and shower facilities port and starboard.

14. Cabins. Fourteen berths were divided between six cabins. Each equipped with a deep lee-cloth to stop occupant falling out when yacht heeled or rolled violently.

15. Storage. Each crew member was allocated three plastic bins to store clothing and effects during each leg. Their shore clothing was air-freighted from port to port.

16. Deckhouse. Chart table surrounded by Autohelm sailing instruments, two Magnavox GPS satellite navigation sets (one linked exclusively to BT's SAT-C satellite tracking system) Raytheon radar screen and Scanti SSB and VHF radios.

17. Galley. Each crew took it in turns to cook. The basic fare was freeze-dried food supplied by MacDougalls supplemented by fresh fruit and vegetables during the first few weeks at sea.

18. Saloon. Large table to seat entire crew sited on opposite side to galley. Cupboard housed IBM computer linked to BT's SAT-C transmission system to send and receive messages and weather data.

19. Skipper/watch leader's cabin. Sited immediately beneath and within earshot of helmsman.

20. Stern lazarette. Storage for fenders and access to steering mechanism.

Original Artwork © Eric North. Computer generation of image © Mark Bosanquet-Bryant & Eric North

The Crew Profiles

BRITISH STEEL II

Skipper

Richard Tudor is a sailmaker by trade with his own business in Pwllheli, North Wales. The 33-year-old, who has skippered a succession of yachts in the UK, Mediterranean and Caribbean and competed in the Three Peaks, Fastnet and Round Ireland races, merely locked the office door when he was given command of British Steel II, and now wants to return to the Southern Ocean, perhaps in the 1993/94 Whitbread race. "I've got unfinished business down there," he says.

Crew

David Arthur (46) Finance broker from Leighton Buzzard, Bedfordshire **Patrick Quinn** (54) Publisher from Didsbury, Manchester **Nigel Bray** (30) Property developer from Grange over Sands, Cumbria.**Kevin Dufficy** (46) Management training consultant from Berkhamstead, Hertfordshire **Marcus Gladwell** (30) Fisherman from Southwold, Suffolk **Michael Martin** (52) Management consultant from Swindon, Wiltshire **Robert Haine** (36) Chartered surveyor from Norwich, Norfolk **Giles Trollope** (44) Company director from London **Steven West** (45) Company director from London **Yvonne Flatman** (31) Trading standards officer from Uxbridge, Middlesex **Michael Sherwood** (48) Electrical engineer from Torquay, Devon.

Leggers

Clare McKernan (28) Technical officer at British Steel's tinplate plant at Swansea (Leg 1) **Michael Smith** (42) Senior shift supervisor from British Steel's plant at Wombourne, West Midlands (Leg 1) **Richard Davies** (30) Shift engineer at British Steel's plant at Deeside, Clwyd (Leg 2) **Louise Broadbent** (26) Salesperson from Bramley, Leeds (Leg 2) **Sandra Hill** (25) Internal auditor at British Steel distribution depot, L:ye, Stourbridge (Leg 3) **Keith Mundell** (33) Design engineer from British Steel plant, Scunthorpe (Leg 3) **Nicola Handley** (26) BS Personnel assistant from Lye Stourbridge (Leg 4) **Harry Heathcock** (45) Senior electrical design engineer from British Steel plant, Lackenby, Worcs (Leg 4).

COMMERCIAL UNION ASSURANCE

Skipper

Will Sutherland (Leg 1), **Richard Merriweather** (Legs 2, 3 & 4). Sutherland (47) was a management training executive before being recruited to the race. He left the yacht at Rio and was replaced by Merriweather, a 27-year-old professional sailor who cut his teeth on the offshore racing circuit before taking command of a sail-training vessel.

Crew

Andrew Stevenson-Hamilton (38) Insurance broker from Edinburgh, Scotland **Roger Boyd** (30) Sales engineer from East Dulwich, London **Stewart Hood** (43) Data processing manager from Otago, New Zealand.**Tony Jones** (54) Company director from Stoke on Trent.**James Kinnier-Wilson** (34) Solicitor from Whaddon, Buckinghamshire.**Mark Lodge** (28) Suspended ceiling fitter from Canvey Island, Essex **Alison McKichan** (30) Market researcher from Edinburgh, Scotland **Jonathan Norton** (24) Insurance broker from South Petherton, Somerset **Sue Tight** (35) Management consultant from Streatham, London **Peter Coop** (36) Sales manager from Oldham, Lancashire **John Gibson** (54) Company director from Newcastle upon Tyne **Eric Gustavson** (52) Plastic surgeon from South Lakenham, Middlesex.

Leggers

Marco Cullen (29) British Steel employee from Caerphilly, Wales (Leg 1) **Vincent Hughes** (26) Production caster from British Steel's Ravenscraig plant in Motherwell, Scotland (Leg 2) **Jonathan Wilson** (29) Electrical engineer at British Steel's plant in Corby (Leg 3) **Keith Taylor** (47) Flooring contractor from Burghfield Common, Reading (Leg 3) **Yvonne Taylor** (46) Accountant, Burghfield Common, Reading (Leg 4) **Dennis Skillicorn** (53) Journalist from Southampton, Hampshire (leg 4).

COOPERS & LYBRAND

Skipper

Vivien Cherry (33) is an engineering services manager with a London-based property company and has a degree in environmental engineering. Her first love, however, is not sewers but sailing, and before this race she had already covered more than 30,000 miles in previous Fastnet races, Scottish and Australian Three Peak events as well as the single-handed Transatlantic race.

Crew

Paul Titchener (30) Accountant from Streatham, London **Matthew Steel-Jessop** (28) Computer network manager from Flitwick, Bedfordshire **Neil Skinner** (34) Heavy goods driver from Salisbury, Wiltshire **Maarten Malmberg** (23) Student from Rotterdam, The Netherlands **Robert Faulds** (30) shop manager from Wemyss Bay, Renfrewshire **Brian Bird** (53) Butcher from Plymouth, Devon **Richard Griffith** (50) Company director from Chiswick, London **David Turner** (33) Financial consultant from Harringay, London **Samantha Wood** (23) Medical student from Brochon, Staffordshire. **Geraint Lewis (30)** Computer analyst from Teddington, Middlesex.

Leggers

Murray Findley (63) Company director from Las Vegas, USA (Leg 1) **Phil Jones** (29) Feeder at British Steel's Tandem Mill at Port Talbot, Wales (Leg 2) **Ann de Boer** (27) PR consultant from Hardenberg, The Netherlands (Legs 1 & 2) **John Kirk** (51) Outdoor activities instructor from Bideford, Devon (Legs 1 & 2) **Gary Hopkins** (36) Local government manager from East Ham, London (Leg 3) **Martin Wright** (35) Investment manager from Helensburgh, Scotland (leg 3) **Shane Dickson** (45) Bank manager from Chandlers Ford, Hampshire (Leg 4) **Paul Shepherd** (40) Maintenance fitter at British Steel's Avesta plant, Sheffield (Leg 4).

GROUP 4 SECURITAS

Skipper

Mike Golding (32) was a watch commander with the fire brigade at Slough, Buckinghamshire before choosing to take on the British Steel Challenge. A sailing instructor in his spare time, he completed his first circumnavigation in 1979 and has competed in several blue-water races including the Azores and Back, Round Britain and single-handed transatlantic events.

Crew

Michael O'Regan (27) Trainee accountant from West Molesey, Surrey **Anthony Marsden** (56) Construction technician from Hong Kong **Nicholas Jubert** (41) Company director from Send, Surrey **Anthony Hill** (28) Dental surgeon from Freshford, Bath **Trevor Harvey** (38) Commissioning engineer from Southampton **Donald Deakin** (53) Company director from Newquay, Cornwall **David Cowan** (53) Lecturer from St Albans, Hertfordshire **Robert Coles** (36) Printer from Aylesbury, Buckinghamshire **Simon Clarke** (28) Company director from London **John Carter** (38) Computer manager from Chalk Farm, London **Gary Ashton** (28) Warehouse manager from Southend-on-Sea, Essex.

Leggers

Simon Littlejohn (31) Freelance photographer from Hammersmith, London (Legs 1, 2, & 3) **Jim Barrett** (40) Group 4 Technical security manager from Broadway, Worcestershire (Leg 1) **Martin Hall** (24) Group 4 cash-in-transit sergeant from Luton, Bedfordshire (Leg 2 & 4) **Keven Handley** (34) Group 4 operations manager from Witham, Essex (Leg 3) **Richard Palmer** (50) Group 4 personnel manager from Evesham, Worcestershire (Leg 4).

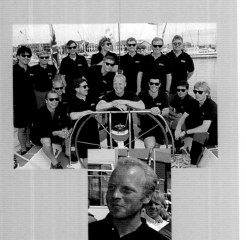

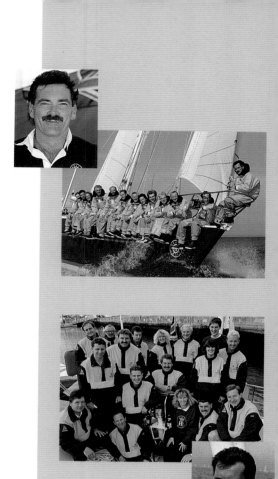

HEATH INSURED
Skipper

Adrian Donovan is a 35-year-old charter yacht skipper from Beadon Park, Devon who graduated from university with an honours degree in nautical studies. A former merchant seaman who rose to the rank of second officer, Donovan has competed in the two-handed transatlantic race and also skippered the winning yacht in the 1991 Trans-Arc race to the West Indies before taking up The Challenge.

Crew

Adrian Arnold (50) Company director from Huntingdon, Cambridgeshire **Samantha Brewster** (25) Outdoor instructor from Windsor, Berkshire **Godfrey Owen** (29) Personnel manager from Lightwater, Surrey **Arthur Haynes** (47) Regional manager from Alum Rock, Birmingham **Kenneth Pearson** (42) Farmer from Dyfed, Wales **Graham Price** (36) Sound engineer from Holland Park, London **Carol Randall** (34) Journalist from Peterborough, Northamptonshire **Adrian Rayson** (36) Company secretary from Henley-on-Thames, Oxfordshire **David Spratley** (29) Sales manager from Datchet Berkshire **William Vincent** (47) Carpenter from Bath, Avon **Stuart Smith-Warren** (45) Senior controller at British Steel's plant at Newport, Gwent **Lisa-Marie Wood** (35) Administrator from Cobham, Surrey.

Leggers

Philip Streeter (32) Turner at British Steel's Avesta plant at Sheffield (Leg 1) **Stephen Stamp** (38) Blast furness engineer at British Steel's plant at Scunthorpe, South Humberside (Leg 2) **Jonathan Goodall** (47) PRO from London (leg 3) **Richard Walker** (26) British Steel chief cashier from Bromford, Worcs (Leg 4).

HOFBRÄU LAGER
Skipper

Pete Goss is a former Royal Marine commando from Torpoint, Cornwall. Before signing up with Chay Blyth to lick his raw recruits into shape, the 31-year-old Green Beret had spent six years working at the Joint Services sail training centre in Plymouth. He is a keen marathon man, having competed in the Round Britain and Scottish Three Peaks events, as well as the single-handed transatlantic race. He is married with two children.

Crew

Andrew Hindley (25) Account manager from Finchley, London **Tristan Lewis** (35) Computer engineer from Powys, Glamorgan **Brian Lister** (62) Insurance broker from Nottingham **Jack Gordon Smith** (45) Market gardener from Cambridge **Jonathan Myers** (29) House physician from London **Roger Pratt** (47) Advertising executive from London **Steve Rigby** (25) Unemployed diver from Brighton, Sussex **Rebecca Slater** (27) Nursery nurse from Falmouth, Cornwall **Mark Steadman** (29) Maintenance manager from Maidenhead, Berkshire **Pippa Welch** (29) Computer programmer from Basingstoke, Hampshire.

Leggers

John Giddings (37) Fitter from Scunthorpe, South Humberside (Leg 1) **Kenneth Ellis** (53) Trout breeder from Tattenhall, Chester (Legs 1 & 4) **Michael Kay** (45) Sales executive with The Challenge Business from Blandford Forum, Dorset (Legs 1, 2, & 4) **James Lees** (29) Buyer from Alresford, Hampshire (Leg 2) **Jim Toseland** (33) Personnel manager from Newport, Gwent (Leg 3) **Tricia Smith** (32) PE teacher from New Maldon, Surrey (Leg 3) **Michael Calvin** (35) Chief sports writer for *The Daily Telegraph* from Eversholt, Bedfordshire (Legs 2, 3 & 4).

INTERSPRAY
Skipper

Paul Jeffes hails from Cove, Dunbartonshire in Scotland where he runs the Silvers Marine boatyard on the Clyde. A qualified naval architect and surveyor, the 40-year-old skipper had previously competed in two Round Britain races, the Scottish three Peaks event and has been a regular competitor on the Scottish offshore racing scene since 1983. In his spare time, he is a lifeboat coxswain.

Crew

Patrick Brockman (30) Advertising executive from Kensington, London **Paul Buchanan** (31) Corporate account manager from Ealing, London **Douglas Gillespie** (26) Estate manager from Kirkcudbright, Dumfries **John Davis** (52) Managing director of a petroleum distributors in New South Wales, Australia **Carlton Dodd** (39) Investment marketing executive from Stratford-upon-Avon, Warwickshire **Dominic Matthews** (48) Managing director of a financial consultancy in Maidstone, Kent **Julian Wells** (42) Vet from Shrewsbury, Shropshire **Alison Smith** (25) Sports psychologist from Thirsk, Yorkshire **Brian Warr** (43) Fitter from Barrow, South Humberside **Jeff Plummer** (45) Oil industry executive from Barton Turf, Norfolk **Richard Scott** (38) Shop floor worker at Courtaulds Fibres, Newcastle **Juliet Connell** (50) Air stewardess from Sittingbourne, Kent.

Leggers

Paul Gelder (46) Features editor of *Yachting Monthly* from Emsworth, Hampshire (Leg 1) **Barry Ford** (31) Engineer at British Steel's Avesta stainless division in Sheffield (leg 2) **Roger Peek** (46) Treasurer of British Steel plc and director of The Challenge Business Ltd (Leg 3) **Ruth Colenso** (26) Graduate trainee from British Steel's Shotton plant on Deeside (Leg 4).

NUCLEAR ELECTRIC
Skipper

John Chittenden is a master mariner with more than 130,000 sea miles to his credit. The 52-year-old former cruising secretary to the Royal Yachting Association skippered the winning cruiser division entry Creighton's Naturally in the 1989/90 Whitbread race. On his return to Southampton at the end of The Challenge, he became the first man to race around the world in both directions.

Crew

John Cox (50) Company director from Hungerford, Berkshire **Christopher Head** (47) Subsea engineer from Christchurch, Dorset **Nicholas Edgington** (35) Computer systems consultant from Slough, Buckinghamshire **Nigel Janes** (22) Ex-student from Woodford Wells, Essex **Roy Meakin** (25) Lifeguard from Long Eaton, Nottingham **John Nash** (42) Building services engineer from Brentford, Middlesex **Richard Rollinshaw** (46) Baker from Brighton, Sussex **John Tillisch** (40) Company director from London **Martin Bayfield** (33) Banking system consultant from St Albans, Hertfordshire.

Leggers

John Pollard (42) Work study assistant from Nuclear Electric's Hartlepool power station, Cleveland (Leg 1) **Neil Stewart** (50) Engineer from Nuclear Electric's Wylfa power station, Anglesey (Leg 1) **David Johnson** (57) Chiropodist from Eastbourne, Sussex (Leg 1) **Steven Yates** (34) Paramedic from Sheffield (Leg 1 & 2) **Liz Macdonald** (35) Administration officer from Nuclear Electric's headquarters at Barnwood, Gloucestershire (Leg 2) **Martin Barker** (31) Mechanical craftsman from Nuclear Electric's Heysham 2 power station, Lancashire (Leg 2) **Nicholas Lupton** (29) Engineer from Nuclear Electric's Sizewell B power station, Suffolk (Leg 3) **Bill Mew** (38) Mechanical craftsman from Nuclear Electric's Dungeness A power station, Romney Marsh, Kent (Leg 2) **Nicholas Marshall** (23) Electrician from Nuclear Electric's Oldbury power station, Avon (Leg 3) **William St Leger** (36) Fire officer from Hobart, Tasmania (Leg 3).**Martin Clarke** (37) Charge hand plant operator from Nuclear Electric's Sizewell A power station, Suffolk (Legs 3 & 4) **Peter Thomas** (54) Production procurements manager from Nuclear Electric's Bristol office (Leg 4) **Douglas Foulds** (31) Instrument mechanic from Nuclear Electric's Heysham 1 power station, Lancashire (Leg 4) **Greta Thomas** (29) Corporate Press officer from Nuclear Electric, London (Leg 4).

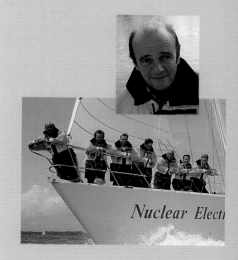

Nuclear Elect

RHÔNE-POULENC

Skipper

Alec Honey (Pre-race training period) **John O'Driscoll** (Leg 1) **Peter Phillips** (Legs 2, 3 & 4) Honey left the yacht three weeks before the start of the race to look after his wife who had fallen ill. He was replaced by Lt Commander John O'Driscoll (49) who was given leave of absence from the Royal Navy to do the race. But he too resigned for personal reasons in Rio. His berth was then filled by Peter Phillips (58) a contemporary of Blyth when both were keen competitors in transatlantic races.

Crew

Simon Walker (25) Property developer from New Milton, Hants **Daniel Sailor** (60) Prison officer (retired) from Lancaster **Justine Cotton** (23) Graduate from Langho, Lancashire **Valerie Elliot** (50) Teacher from Leicester **Suzanne Emerson** (29) Computer programmer from Acton, London **Nicholas Fenner** (27) Solicitor from Hong Kong **Anthony Fowler** (42) Property developer from Westbury, Kent (Leg 1) **Steven George** (43) Revenue purchasing manager from Waterinberry, Kent **Jerry Walshingham** (37) Sales manager from Raynes Park, London **Campbell MacKenzie** (58) Renal surgeon (retired) from Bristol **Rod Street** (45) Property renovator from Gloucester **David Brydon** (29) Futures trader from Hindhead, Surrey.

Leggers

Jane Laycock (28) Process technician from Eastbourne, Sussex (Leg 1) **John Haynes** (51) Solicitor from Hong Kong **Angus MacKenzie** (24) Printer from Bristol (Leg 2) **Paul Egan** (27) electronics engineer from Frimley, Surrey (Legs 2, 3 & 4) **Nicholas Atha** (37) Tanker driver from Sheffield (Leg 3) **Steven George** (43) Revenue purchasing manager from Waterinberry, Kent (leg 4).

PRIDE OF TEESSIDE

Skipper

Ian MacGillivray has been at one with the sea since leaving school. The 36-year-old from Southampton qualified as a dinghy instructor at 16 before graduating as a boatbuilder. Now a professional yacht skipper, he made two transatlantic crossings in his own yacht in 1985, and in the year before The Challenge, shared the task of training Blyth's crew volunteers with Pete Goss.

Crew

John Bagley (55) Agronomist from Godalming, Surrey **Gary Bailey** (45) Company director from Chelmsford, Essex **Andrew Chamberlain** (23) Satellite scientist from Farnborough, Hampshire **Les Dickinson** (48) Holiday apartment manager from Skegness **Ramin Dilmaghanian** (24) Civil structural engineer from St Johns Wood, London **Helen Griffiths** (21) Graduate from Gwynedd, North Wales **Philip Harvey** (27) Investment assistant from Kingston-upon-Thames, Surrey **Robert Milnes** (28) Doctor from New Kendal, Cumbria **Kate Twyman** (27) Software engineer from Faversham, Kent **David Willbank** (34) Company director from Surbiton, Surrey. **Richard Oliver** (55) Baker from Wadebridge, Cornwall **John Hooper** (42) Solicitor from Brent Knoll, Somerset.

Leggers

David Donkin (31) BS accident prevention manager from Cleveland (Leg 1) **Sue McKichan** (32) Researcher from Edinburgh, Scotland (Legs 2, 3, & 4) **Keith Snell** (44) BS fabricator from Llanwern, Gwent (Legs 2 & 3) **George Backhouse** (57) Retired farmer from the Algarve, Portugal (leg 3&4) **Ian Bibby** (29) Engineer from Thirsk, Yorkshire (Leg 4) **Beverley Mulvenna** (33) Corporate lawyer from London (Leg 4).

CHAPTER THREE

"Rolling Down to Rio"

A Transatlantic
Shakedown Cruise

The final week before the start was

inevitably tinged with a good deal of apprehension. Crews, skippers, friends, relatives - everyone was in Southampton's Ocean Village to lend a hand with the final victualling, including the one-leggers, many of whom would not see their crew mates again until the fleet arrived in Rio, Hobart or Cape Town.

There were also the inevitable late changes with which to contend. Two crew, both Names at Lloyds, bailed out to rebuild their lives after losing their shirts in the City insurance crash. A slipped disc forced another to throw in the towel; one could not raise the final instalment on the £15,000 payment for the voyage, while a third was given the fateful news that his wife had cancer and decided to stay at home to comfort her.

One spare berth was filled at short notice by Steven Yates, an intensive care nurse from Sheffield, who answered a call in The Times two days before the start for a medic to join Nuclear Electric. The 34-year-old had raced with Nuclear Electric's skipper John Chittenden in the Whitbread Round the World Race aboard Creighton's Naturally two years before and had only just returned from cruising round the world on the same yacht. A sucker for punishment, he was the obvious choice, and though he signed on for the first leg only, Yates stayed until Hobart.

John Hayes, a barrister from Hong Kong, had read about the Challenge while passing through London just a month before the start. He rang Blyth's office on the off-chance that a place might become available at the 11th hour. One did, and he was on the first flight back to England to sail the initial leg aboard the Rhône-Poulenc with its new skipper John O'Driscoll.

Even the bookies got in on the act. They were not so much taking bets on how many more would fall by the wayside, but setting the odds on the yachts themselves, based on their performance in the Fastnet race. Initial odds posted by William Hill placed Hofbräu Lager the 3:1 favourite;

The fleet at Ocean Village, Southampton. Left: Richard Tudor's crew bid farewell

British Steel II and Rhône-Poulenc second at 7:2; followed by InterSpray 4:1; Nuclear Electric 6:1; Coopers & Lybrand, Group 4 and Heath Insured 16:1; Pride of Teesside at 20:1.

Commercial Union stood at 33:1. The bookies had obviously picked up a few inside tips, for the crew were not a happy bunch. No one could come to terms with skipper Will Sutherland's confrontational style of management, or his reluctance to delegate responsibility. Most of the crew blamed this for their poor performance in the Fastnet race. The issue came to a head on the eve of the race when Blyth was forced to confront Sutherland at a meeting with the crew. They wanted him replaced, but it was not an option that appealed to Commercial Union which had centred its sponsorship promotions around him.

In the pep-talk that followed, Blyth persuaded the rebels to give their man another chance. He told Sutherland that a good start the following morning was his big opportunity to prove himself. Thus were the problems resolved in the short term, but they did not go away; not by any means.

Vivien Cherry was another to suffer on that final day, though this time with a bad bout of flu. Cherry, the only woman skipper in the race, had been forced to endure more than her share of the pre-race publicity. All day she kept her head down, which caused some concern, but her crew reassured everyone. "It's just nerves. She will be all right on the day," they agreed.

Blyth too was showing signs of strain. After pushing one journalist in the drink that week, the rest of the press corps kept

Rhône-Poulenc was skippered by John O'Driscoll on the first leg. He was then replaced at Rio by former policeman Peter Phillips for the remainder of the race.
Inset: 2,000 boats saw the start from the Solent in perfect conditions

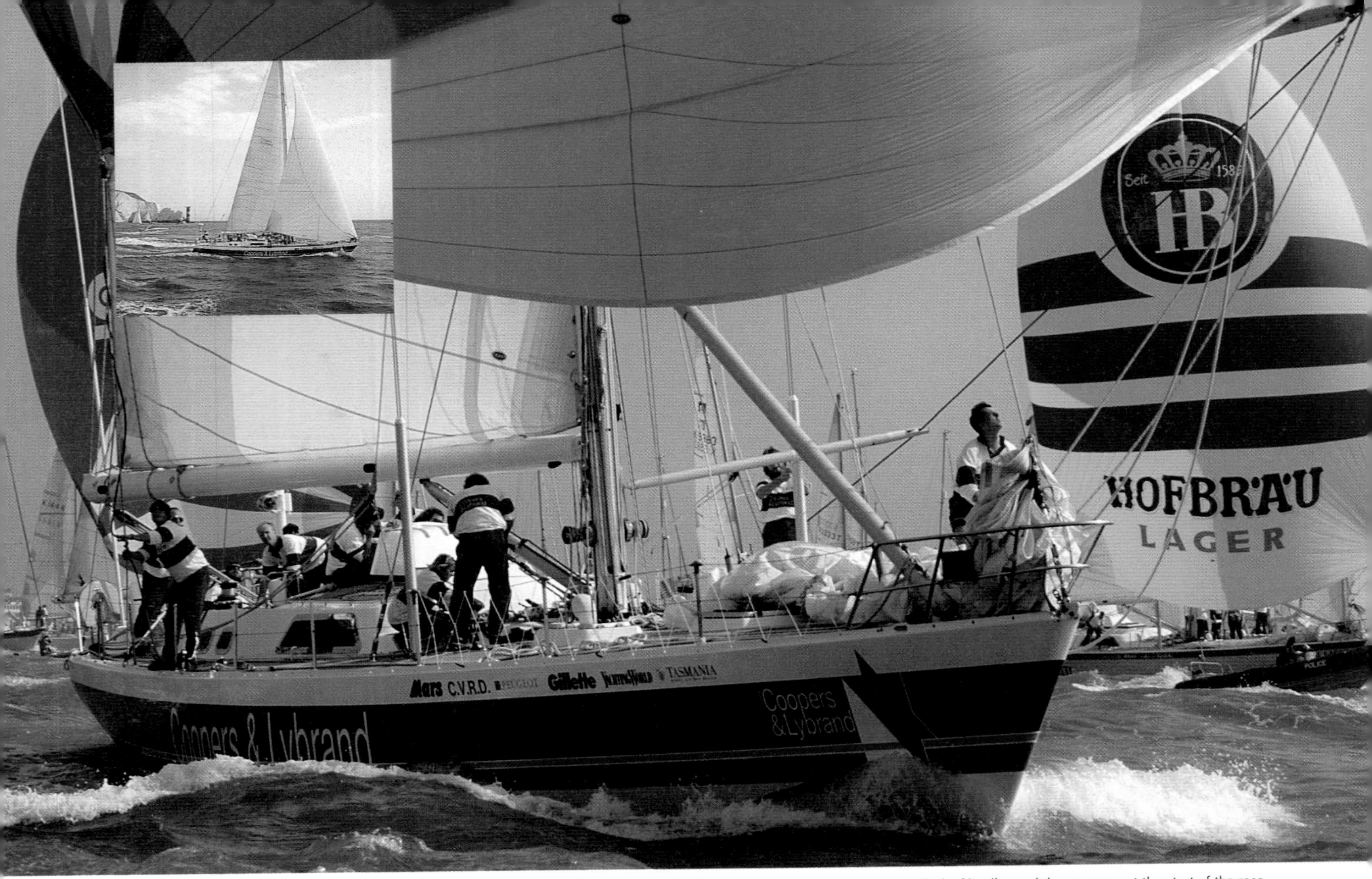
HOFBRÄU
LAGER
Coopers & Lybrand
Coopers
&Lybrand
Mars C.V.R.D.
Gillette
TASMANIA

Running the gauntlet: the crews of Coopers & Lybrand, Hofbräu Lager and British Steel II battle through the spectator fleet towards the Needles and the open sea at the start of the race. There were prizes for the first to reach Lee-on-Solent and Cowes. Inset: Coopers was first to break into the Channel

their distance - and their backs to the water's edge. "I feel a bit like a spare part. I wish I was competing with these crews, not waving them off," said this poacher-turned-gamekeeper as the pressures inexorably mounted.

The day of the start could not have been better. A light easterly breeze cleared away the early morning mist as the Solent slowly filled with spectator craft. By midday the haze had all but burnt away, encouraging more than 2,000 boats, ranging from canoes and jet-skis to sailboats and gin-palaces, to join the throng of harbour and cross-Channel ferries. Thousands more looked on from ashore, standing shoulder to shoulder from Gilkicker Point to Lee-on-Solent. Others lined Cowes Green or provided crews with a final wave from either side of Hurst Narrows as the fleet swept out of the Solent.

> *"I feel a bit like a spare part. I wish I was competing with these crews, not waving them off."*

It was an awesome gauntlet to run, particularly for crews with little or no experience of racing. To add to their difficulties the start was delayed five minutes to accommodate the needs of the BBC's live radio commentary. The delay caught the spectator fleet unawares, causing havoc for the harassed marshals charged with clearing a 500-yard track to the first turning mark.

They were not the only victims of the delay. The hapless Will Sutherland made a perfect run for the line, only to find his timing was five minutes out. "He lost his composure completely, screaming at all of us before retreating below to the chart table," recalled one of his crew when Commercial Union finally arrived at Rio.

By the time all on board appreciated the mistake, they had already doused the headsail, had a spinnaker half hoisted and were left drifting helplessly away on the fierce-running ebb tide. For Sutherland, it was the beginning of the end.

The highly-charged atmosphere also got to Berkshire fireman Mike Golding and his Group 4 Securitas crew. They shot the line ten seconds early, then found it impossible to re-round the outer distance mark as the rules prescribed because Heath Insured had it snagged around her rudder and was dragging it down the Solent to pantomime calls of "It's behind you...!" from laughing spectators. With a mass of other boats converging on the hapless yacht to witness the comic scene, Golding wisely kept clear and turned to follow the fleet without answering the recall.

Commercial Union's crew also did their best to stem the strong current and flow of exuberant spectator craft, but failed to re-cross the line completely. Like Group 4 they too faced the prospect of a time penalty when they reached Rio a month later.

Richard Tudor and his crew on British Steel II made the best start, but found their pace slowed by a split hose-pipe that flooded the boat. "We couldn't understand why we were so sluggish until we lifted up the floor boards and found six inches of water swilling around in the bilges," Tudor reported later.

The early running was then taken up by Nuclear Electric and Pride of Teesside. They led the charge down the Solent almost neck-and-neck. To add spice to the start, Blyth had offered a £2,000 purse to the first crew to pass through a gate off Lee-on-Solent, and another £2,000 bounty for the first through a second off Cowes.

The canny MacGillivray pulled a fast one on the fleet by calling for Teesside's gossamer white lightweight spinnaker which was much better suited to the conditions than the heavily branded, bullet-proof chutes his rivals had felt duty bound to hoist for the sake of their sponsors. As a result, the Teesside crew pipped Nuclear Electric at both gates by little more than the length of their pulpit, leaving Chittenden's men less than content with picking up the secondary prizes.

Poulenc (*French* puⅼɛɪk) n. **Francis** (frãsis). 1899-1963, French composer; a member of Les Six, son of Emile Poulenc, founder of the company *Poulenc Frères*, which later became *Rhône-Poulenc*.

Rhône-Poulenc, from *Rhône* (rəʊn) mighty French river, and *Poulenc* (puⅼɛɪk), famous French composer.
Together, one of the world's leaders in the fields of healthcare, chemicals, agriculture and fibres. Rhône-Poulenc operates from 30 locations in the UK with a workforce of over 5000. Globally, some 90,000 people are employed by Rhône-Poulenc in 140 countries.

Adapted from The Collins English Dictionary.

RHÔNE-POULENC

OAK HOUSE REEDS CRESCENT WATFORD WD1 1QH
TEL: 0923 211700 TLX: 911536 RPCHEM G FAX: 0923 211580

Photo Christel clear

Yachts and Yachting
covers every aspect of the CHS scene. For informed comment and topical coverage order from your newsagent now.

196 Eastern Esplanade, Southend-on-Sea, Essex SS1 3AB. Tel: (0702) 582245; Fax: (0702) 588434

At the western end of the Solent a gusting wind funnelling through Hurst Narrows caught out several crews. Coopers & Lybrand's crew were among the first to recover their composure - and spinnaker - and were rewarded with the lead as the fleet headed out past the Needles. MacGillivray, who had Bob Fisher, the Guardian's yachting correspondent standing alongside looking suspiciously like a tactician, chose to steer Pride of Teesside through the North Channel, close under Hurst Castle, and keep the spinnaker flying. This inshore course would also

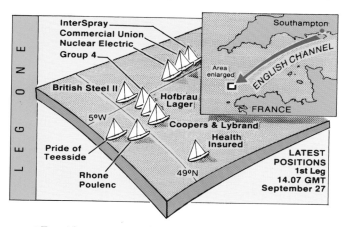

put Teesside at a greater advantage when the tide turned against the fleet later, lifting her crew into first place with an 18-mile lead over the last-placed yachts Commercial Union and InterSpray when the first of BT's satellite position reports was published after three hours of racing.

If Fisher, who was on board to wax lyrically on the race for a live radio programme, had proffered local advice in these his home waters, he got his just desserts, because the photo-boat crew charged with picking him up did not locate Teesside hidden under the cliffs at Anvil Point on the Dorset coast until almost dusk. "I was beginning to think you had forgotten me," said the much relieved broadcaster when the inflatable finally came alongside. We didn't have the heart to tell him we had.

After this light-air introduction, crews got a first taste of what was to come when they ran into the tail of Hurricane Charlie while crossing the Bay of Biscay. With winds gusting up to 45 knots, they were given such a hammering that many fell seasick. Hofbräu Lager reported losing a jockey pole and two winch handles, a sail tore on Teesside and a wave swept John Davis off his feet aboard InterSpray, leaving him bruised and battered against the dorade hatch. Carol Randall slipped and hit her head while scrambling below decks aboard Heath Insured during the height of the gale. She had to wear a neck brace for the rest of the voyage.

Midway across Biscay, MacGillivray's crew held a tenuous five-mile lead over British Steel II. Tudor's crew had fixed the leak by now but were slowed momentarily when the yacht rammed a basking shark, which "went off in a sulk" according to Giles Trollope, the navigator. He also reported two visitors on board - a large moth and a small yellowhammer. "The bird ate the moth, had a kip in the skipper's bunk, then flew off. Richard thought our spinnaker had torn and called for it to be doused, only to find that the bird had deposited a dropping on the sail as it left us."

Another rising star was Heath Insured. Stung perhaps by their mark-towing spectacle at the start, Donovan and his team had pulled back through the fleet and were now challenging

Hofbräu Lager for third place. The loser that day was Rhône-Poulenc which slipped from second to sixth, dropping 29 miles behind Teesside.

Teesside's torn genoa eventually cost her first place as the crew struggled to stitch it by hand, but greatest concern was for Commercial Union. Seventy-eight miles behind the leader British Steel II, and well to the west of the fleet, she appeared to lie hove-to overnight. How could one boat fall so far behind a one-design fleet that was providing such close racing? The answer would not become clear until the finish.

From Cape Finisterre onwards, however, this 5,300-mile initiation turned into "something of a Caribbean cruise", as one crewman described it when the fleet rolled into Rio the following month. Many had sailed with spinnakers set for more than half the voyage.

But whatever they lost in terms of heavy weather experience was more than made up for by the tight racing. Positions changed continually. On day five, for instance, British Steel II slipped back to third as Teesside took up the running once more, with Hofbräu in sight, three miles astern. The Nuclear Electric crew had also begun to make their presence felt, moving up four places to fourth, bringing InterSpray and Group 4 in her wake.

Those to lose ground were Vivien Cherry's crew on Coopers & Lybrand who slipped two places to seventh; Rhône-Poulenc which slumped to eighth and Heath Insured which slipped back to ninth after all had been forced to tack westwards to clear Finisterre.

Heath Insured crewman Adrian Rayson summed up the changing moods on board. "The expected south-easterlies failed

> *"The bird ate the moth, had a kip in the skipper's bunk, then flew off."*

Commercial Union plunges to windward, a crew mutiny bubbling below the surface

to appear, leaving us too far into the Bay of Biscay, and a frustrating tack westwards deadened the mood until we turned south and had our bows pointing towards Rio once more."

"Problems at home, those emotional goodbyes and the euphoria of the start are all behind us. So too are the dissenting voices of those who say we are mad. Maybe we are, but already it has become a thrilling, testing madness. The last two nights have been moonless, black and rough, calling for constant reefing and

Mike Martin, a management consultant from Swindon. Sitting on the weather rail of British Steel II, he told Kevin Dufficy confidentially how much he was missing his Canadian girl-friend, Carol McBean. "I really must make an honest women out of her," Martin told him quietly. "Well, why not put a call through on the radio and tell her" was Dufficy's advice. He did, and after repeating the proposal four times for the video cameraman, Carol and the entire listening nautical world knew

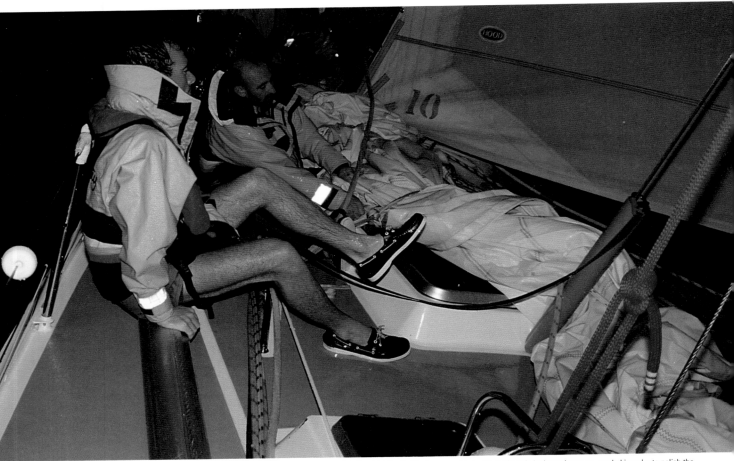

Night watches: the crew of Interspray drag yet another wet sail down during a balmy night in mid-Atlantic. The leg proved to be the perfect shakedown the crews needed in order to polish the skills they had learnt in training, but the real weather was yet to come

headsail changes. The days have been clear but with light fluky winds frustrating sail-trimmers and helmsmen alike. The crew have shaken down well but dark fears loom at testing times."

The same line was taken by Sue Tight aboard CU whose hopes of their extreme westerly course paying off had now begun to dim. "Half the crew have become very religious after various bouts on the foredeck, where they have become well and truly christened. Also, many things are not taken for granted any more: getting dressed, hot running water, eight hours sleep, dry clothes - and the value of £15,000!"

Another problem that all the teams were trying desperately to resolve was the computerised weather fax system for receiving the all-important mapped forecasts. Paul Jeffes and his crew on InterSpray finally received an image on their screen, but the broken isobar lines prompted one crewman to report back to race control: "They seem as much help as asking Michael Fish which day of summer is best for a barbecue."

One man who couldn't quite cut his ties with home was

about his feelings. Within a trice, a date was set in Rio and Chay Blyth was roped in to give the blushing bride away!

By 2 October, the fleet had fanned out over a 150-mile area in an attempt to find a path through the calms that had descended off the Portuguese coast. One crew to benefit was InterSpray which moved up eight places in as many hours to take the lead away from Teesside and Hofbräu. Jeffes and his crew had gained their jump by keeping close to the coast and picking up the local land and sea breezes. Reporting their good fortune, Jeffes said: "I am not comfortable being so exposed on the outer edge of the fleet, in case something develops out to the west, but there is nothing interesting on the weather maps, so we will continue to live dangerously."

Pete Goss put Hofbräu's sudden ill-fortune down to their lack of weather information. "Ocean racing is a game of chess, but without the weatherfax, we can see only half the board," he complained.

Three days later, the fickle conditions helped Vivien

Cherry's Coopers & Lybrand to make an equally impressive run through the fleet. The first Jeffes knew of the challenge was when an unidentified light was spotted shortly after mid-night as InterSpray closed on Madeira. It turned out to be Cooper's masthead light, and at 3am Cherry called her rival up on the radio saying: "I think it's time to take the yellow jersey. By my calculations, we are ahead!"

In a remarkable run, the Coopers crew had clawed back more than 40 miles in the space of a day by making the most of a private 25-knot north-westerly wind off the Moroccan coast. They were now the fifth yacht to lead the fleet since the start of the race ten days earlier. Jeffes appeared unperturbed by this sudden reversal. "It's nice to have company out here, but it is a question of playing the course or the weather, and right now we are playing the weather. I'm in the business of beating her over the next 5,000 miles, not the next five minutes."

Ninety miles astern, the crew on Heath Insured laid claim to a record run of 245.1 miles noon-to-noon between 3-4 October. Despite the excitement, they could not improve on their eighth place.

Adrian Rayson, summed up most feelings within the fleet when he wrote in his log: "Two weeks into the British Steel Challenge and only now has it begun to sink in that there is no turning back. The adventure has actually begun. We are bowling along at 10 knots with the wind up the chuff and a hint of a smile about our skipper's face. Crew morale has varied since the start and some of us were sick in the Bay of Biscay. In those darkest moments, one or two allowed themselves to think this is a terrible mistake but, no doubt, this bashing and the emotional troughs are a rehearsal for the mighty Southern Ocean to come."

Stitch in time: sail-mending was all by hand as no sewing machines were taken. Irreparable sail damage incurred a stiff penalty

"It has also started to sink in that 67ft is a very small environment in which to spend several weeks with 13 others. Arthur Haynes spoke of walking to the pub for a pint before dinner this evening and it seemed a very good idea!"

Rayson's mood was in stark contrast to the depression descending on Commercial Union, now dragging her stern more than 100 miles behind the leaders on a lonely course well west of the fleet. Talking in Rio, Alison McKichan told of the frustrations that built up to pressure-cooker proportions within the yacht. "The skipper had done a lot of preparation on routeing and had decided we should sail well to the west. It didn't pay off at all and during those first two weeks, we had nine days when we didn't have more than five knots of wind and went from one

hole into another."

The crew mumbled about the need to head east and were backed up by Jim Kinnier-Wilson, the navigator on board. But Sutherland was not for turning. He ignored them all.

The building pressure finally blew the lid off the pot one October day, two weeks into the voyage. After waiting for Sutherland to fall asleep, Sue Tight went to the computer and fired off a coded plea to Blyth calling for his dismissal. The message read: "Situation disgust at Baden Powell House remains unchanged. Please carry out your promise, No reply possible." The mutinous message was signed by the entire crew.

CU's Alison McKichan, dressed for the Equator

Back in Petersfield, Blyth, who had suspected the worst by the way the yacht was performing, moved hastily. First he checked through his list of reserves to earmark another skipper, then he broke the bad news to Commercial Union, the sponsor. No one outside this close-knit group - least of all Sutherland - would know of this mutiny until the yacht was closing on Rio three weeks later.

Another crew with troubles to contend with for the rest of the voyage was Rhône-Poulenc. They had been shredding and mending spinnakers all week while others carried theirs non-stop. As a result they had dropped disappointedly back in line with Commercial Union. Determined not to throw the remnants away and incur a possible penalty for losing a sail, the crew formed a sewing circle and spent the next week re-stitching the sail from head to foot. After this marathon session, John Haynes wrote in his log: "There is nothing cosmetic about this surgical repair - 100ft of double hand-stitched laceration cannot be disguised. The task seemed impossible, working round the clock in shifts, frequently by torch light on a heaving deck. The job was done in five days and is now drawing 41 tons of yacht at speeds that sometimes exceed 11 knots."

> *"There is nothing cosmetic about this surgical repair - 100ft of double hand-stitched laceration cannot be disguised."*

"Who is responsible for this minor miracle? A skipper, a mate and 12 crew members who have decided not to ditch the tattered sail. It would be repaired. The task was huge. The skipper's company became a human sewing machine. One watch zigged and the other zagged. The fleet's doctor put in more stitches in five days than a hospital sees in five years. Lieutenant commander, mate, carpenter, prison officer, process technician, airport manager and barrister sewed as if their lives depended on it. And they sewed well because all the stitches had to pass muster with the our sail mistress, primary school teacher Valerie Elliott."

"This simple, giant enterprise was tough. But you talk while you sew and it was fun. The team sewed itself together and the miracle is that it worked. Small wonder that a modest cheer broke out as the scarred spinnaker shook herself out, collected the wind and headed for Rio. Rhône-Poulenc was back in the race!"

Surprisingly, the inshore course down the African coast continued to pay, and once Adrian Donovan decided to take this easterly route, the gamble lifted Heath Insured five places to third and within seven miles of British Steel II. "They were very lucky," conceded John O'Driscoll. "Sailing to leeward of both the Canary and Cape Verde Islands is against all the advice in the sailing books, but they got away with it - and good luck to them."

Gamble or not, the unexpected absence of trade winds in the Northern Hemisphere turned this leg into a three-horse race as InterSpray, British Steel II and Heath headed for the Equator, often within sight of each other. The North-East Trades may not have materialised, but whichever was first to find the South-East Trades was likely to make the best time.

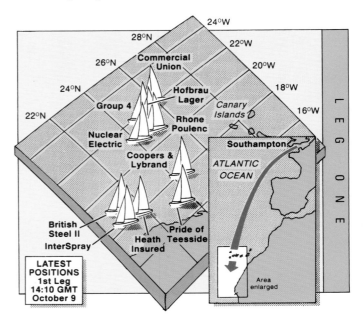

On 11 October, 16 days into the race, the lead remained finally balanced. British Steel II held a tenuous two-mile advantage over InterSpray as these two steered a course midway between Senegal and Cape Verde, leaving Heath Insured 50 miles adrift on the west side of the islands.

But nine days of running under spinnaker can soften reflexes in the best crew, a fact borne out aboard British Steel II with almost disastrous consequences when crewman Rob Haine lost the tip of his thumb in a freak accident. The 36-year-old Australian surveyor had been tying a spinnaker trip-line to the yacht's toe-rail when someone tripped the guy accidentally from around the cockpit winch. His thumb became trapped in the loop of the bowline by the sudden tension. As the load went on the line, Haine let out a piercing scream, fell to the deck and rolled around clutching his fingers. "There was so much blood, we thought he must have lost his entire hand," one crewman recalled.

> "I injected one side OK, but when I touched the other, the needle must have hit a nerve because he nearly shot through the cabin roof."

The team rallied round to give him first-aid, following advice proffered before the race by Dr Campbell MacKenzie, the senior medical officer within the fleet. The job of administering a local anaesthetic fell to Marcus Gladwell, a Suffolk fisherman whose previous medical experience was limited to a few days spent on a training course before the race. Haine was his first patient.

Unable to raise a doctor within the fleet by radio, Gladwell selected a medium-sized needle and a regular dosage of painkiller from the yacht's extensive medical kit and set about administering his first injection. "I was more nervous than Rob and had to turn away to stop myself from shaking," Gladwell remembered. "I injected one side OK, but when I touched the other, the needle must have hit a nerve because he nearly shot through the cabin roof."

But Gladwell's Florence Nightingale act soon took effect, reducing the searing pain to a dull throb. "My greatest concern was not my thumb, but the fact that the injury might put me out of the race," said Haine, whose condition was monitored over the radio by Julian Wells, the vet aboard InterSpray. "Is his nose wet? - keep giving him the Bob Martin's" became the stock joke, but it was not long before the patient was up and about again. He even managed a smile when, with typical black humour, his

crew mates gave the tip of his thumb "a decent burial at sea" after finding it still embedded in the knot.

Sixteen days into the race and the battle for first place was just as intense. That day the lead changed three times as first InterSpray, then British Steel II gained an edge from the wind. Tudor, who also reported hitting a shark, said: "This tussle is very exciting. We are often in sight of each other and had our nose ahead for the past day or so."

Four hundred miles to the north-west another duel had developed for the middle order placings between Rhône-Poulenc, Nuclear Electric, Hofbräu Lager and Group 4. The most remarkable performance, however, came from Coopers & Lybrand. Vivien Cherry had decided to follow the leaders to leeward of the Cape Verde Islands. Her crew set the fastest pace that day, and though trailing 330 miles behind the leading trio, the day's run lifted Coopers four places to sixth.

After trading gybes and insults for three days, the crews on InterSpray and British Steel II ran into the Doldrums on 14 October, giving Donovan's team on Heath a chance to close the gap. Sailing a little more to the west, Heath closed up to within 14 miles of InterSpray, and broke ahead of British Steel II when Tudor chose to gybe and try his luck at crossing the Equator further east. It was a handy move, for when the trio crossed the "Line" three days later, it was British Steel II that held the lead.

King Neptune visited each in turn to perform the timeless ritual of baptising each novice in turn with some vile concoction.

Some crews, more interested in racing than ritual, limited the fun to a hasty toast. Those on InterSpray and Coopers & Lybrand went to great lengths to ensure a memorable "crossing". These fun and games were a good way of letting off the steam that built up aboard all the yachts in the hot-house

THE CARFAX AWARD FOR
THE BRITISH STEEL CHALLENGE
ROUND THE WORLD
YACHT RACE

Carfax Publishing Company has invited the individual crew
members from all ten yachts to write a report describing the
inspiration and personal achievements they have gained from their
participation in the British Steel Challenge.
The winner will be chosen by the directors of Carfax Publishing
Company and awarded this superb, specially created trophy.
A similar award has been commissioned for the best report written
by a yacht skipper describing the development and progression of
his crew during this tough and exciting round the world race.

CARFAX PUBLISHING COMPANY
International Periodical Publishers
PO Box 25, Abingdon, Oxfordshire OX14 3UE,
United Kingdom.
Telephone: 0235 555335 Fax: 0235 553559

PO Box 2025,Dunnellon,Florida 34430-2025,USA.

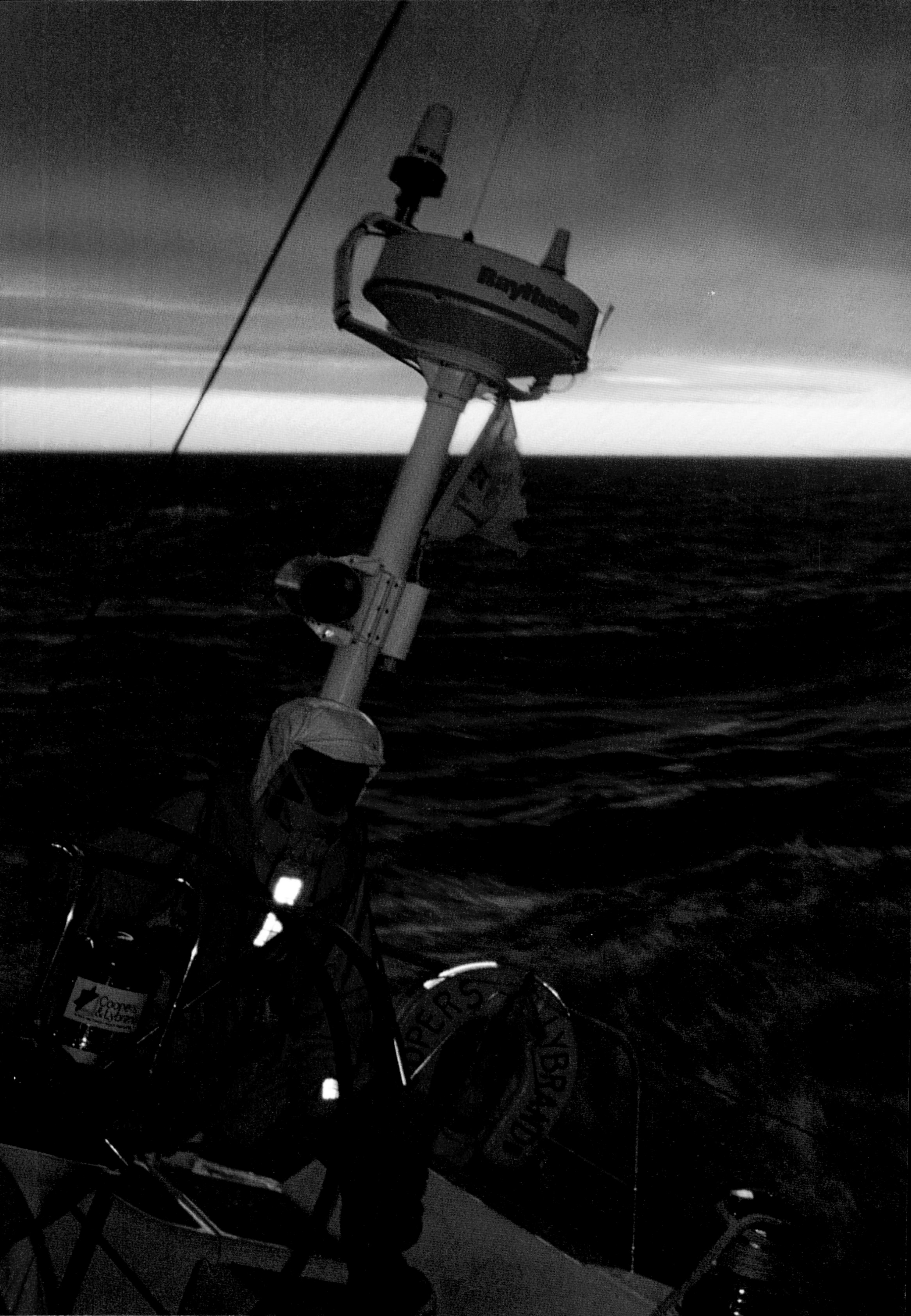
Raytheon

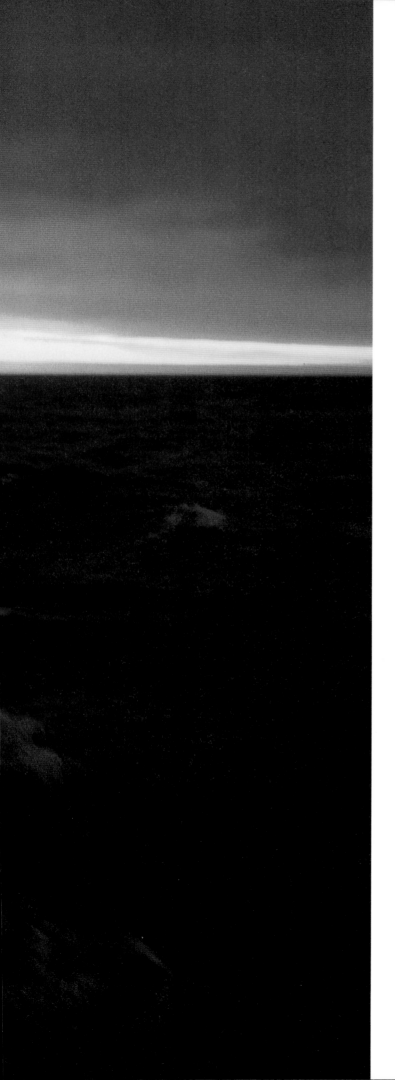

Aspects of life on the ocean wave: a sunset, seen from Coopers & Lybrand, a meal-time chat before another watch begins on Heath Insured and trying skills at halyard riding in mid ocean. This was what the crews had saved so hard to experience

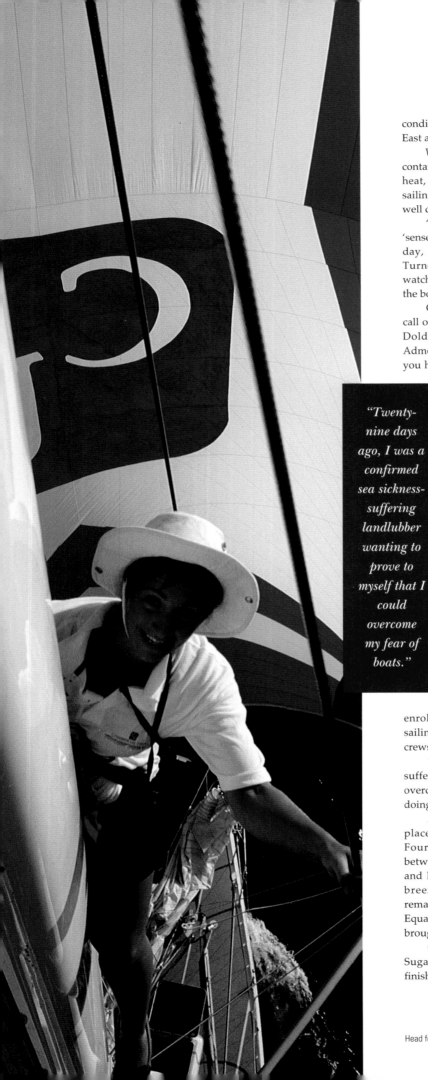

conditions that prevail in the horse latitudes dividing the North-East and South-East Trades.

Writing in The Times, Vivien Cherry told how they contained the problem on Coopers & Lybrand: "With the rising heat, tempers can get short. Add some slow and frustrating sailing, mix with 14 people, bake inside a steel hull and stand well clear."

"Standing clear is not an option, so instead we have a 'sense of humour failure' board. Only two failures are allowed a day, and each is marked out of ten. Top of the list is David Turner, when inadvertently woken two hours early for his watch. After the comments and the inevitable cartoon (drawn on the board) he was all smiles again."

Geraint Lewis won another prize for services beyond the call of duty. Cleaning the topsides of Coopers & Lybrand in the Doldrums, he inadvertently dropped his brush overboard. Admonished by his skipper with words to the effect of: "Well, you had better go and get it", he dived overboard and swam to retrieve it. Cherry could not believe her eyes, but this mock man-overboard incident turned to reality when Lewis found that he could not swim fast enough to catch up with the yacht again. "We were hardly moving," recalled Cherry. "But two knots of current were running and he just couldn't make it back. We eventually had to drop the spinnaker and turn back. We probably lost about an hour, but the one good thing was that it made all the crew much more safety conscious."

Lewis was forced to wear the brush on a lanyard round his neck for a few days as a reminder.

Once into the southern latitudes, British Steel II slowly pulled away from her rivals, crossing the finish line off Copacabana beach on Sunday 26 October, some ten hours ahead of InterSpray. As the champagne flowed, Tudor congratulated his crew. "It's an amazing achievement - exactly what we dreamt of for so long. I just find it hard to believe it has actually happened."

Clare McKernan, a 28-year-old technical officer at British Steel's Trostre plant in Swansea, and one of the one-leggers aboard, was just as ecstatic as her skipper picked up the Infolink Trophy. "When I first enrolled on the Challenge three years ago, I had never been sailing. Now I have raced over 5,300 miles against nine other crews - and won!"

"Twenty-nine days ago, I was a confirmed sea sickness-suffering landlubber wanting to prove to myself that I could overcome my fear of boats. This is a pretty spectacular way of doing it."

Adrian Donovan's Heath Insured crew were secure in third place, thanks to a 230-mile cushion on the rest of the fleet. Fourth place, however, turned into an extraordinary duel between Group 4 Securitas, Hofbräu Lager, Pride of Teesside and Nuclear Electric - thanks in part to the notoriously fickle breezes that invariably prevail around Rio. This quartet remained close for the better part of a week after crossing the Equator, but it was the vagaries of Copacabana Bay that finally brought them together.

Golding's crew were the first to sight Rio's famous Sugarloaf mountain, but ran out of wind within sight of the finish, giving the chasing crews an opportunity to close the gap.

"Twenty-nine days ago, I was a confirmed sea sickness-suffering landlubber wanting to prove to myself that I could overcome my fear of boats."

Head for heights: Sue Tight tests her nerve up the mast of Commercial Union

Chores: meals were the highpoint of the day, even if
the food became monotonous

Flying meals: the ubiquitous flying fish which came aboard throughout the voyage made a
welcome change to the diet of freeze-dried food

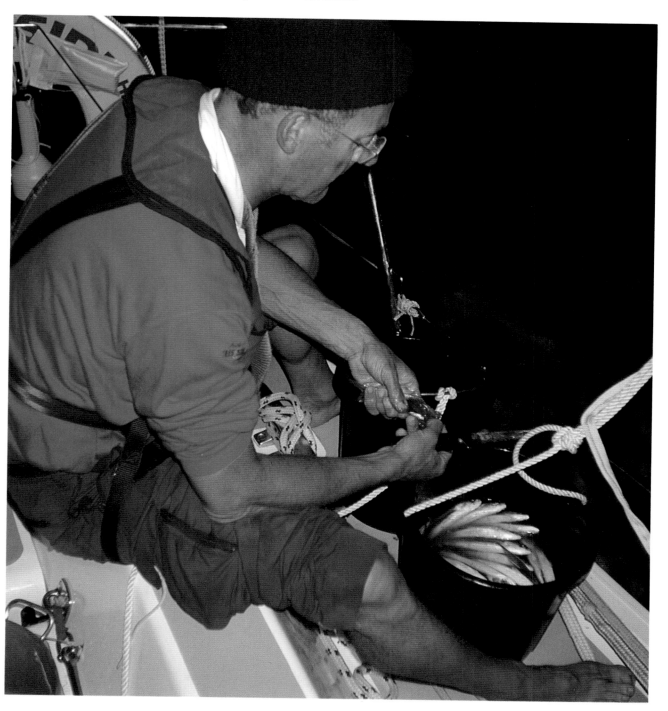

Close run thing: after 5,000 miles racing, just two minutes separated Pride of Teesside from Hofbräu Lager as Rio hove into view. Group 4 Securitas, remarkably, finished between them. The final hours of the leg were nerve-wracking, as crews saw hard-fought leads evaporate off Copacabana

They took it with open arms.

Initially, it looked to onlookers as if Hofbräu Lager would take greatest advantage of Group 4's windless plight, but the dice finally rolled in Teesside's favour. MacGillivray and his crew chased every zephyr to sneak across the line 59 seconds ahead of Golding's men. Hofbräu finished sixth, a further one minute 52 seconds astern, her crew just as elated as the rest. "That was fantastic," said a smiling Pete Goss. "I'm not disappointed at finishing third. It was just wonderful to be part of a piece of yachting history. I've had only two hours' sleep during the past two days, but my heart rate is just as high now as it was when we started back in the Solent with thousands of boats around us."

That night, John Chittenden and his crew on Nuclear Electric faced an almost identical dilemma to Group 4 in holding off late challenges from Rhône-Poulenc and Coopers & Lybrand. After struggling for 12 hours to cover the last five miles, the former Whitbread race skipper admitted: "Seeing those two spinnakers charging over the dawn horizon was frightening."

Crewman John Tillisch agreed. "The last 24 hours were certainly a bit of a paradox. First we blew two spinnakers out in 30 knots of wind, then sat at anchor totally becalmed for the next 11 hours." The wind filled in just in time and, after struggling on the foredeck to get the hook up, the Nuclear crew ghosted across the line 12 minutes ahead of Rhône-Poulenc, followed eight minutes later by Coopers & Lybrand.

> *"First we blew two spinnakers out in 30 knots of wind, then sat at anchor totally becalmed for the next 11 hours."*

Commercial Union finally hove into sight in the early dawn six days later. It had been a disastrous voyage. While the crew danced on deck as they crossed the line, their skipper Will Sutherland remained a lonely figure at the stern. Once he had been taken ashore, those who had stayed up all night to welcome CU were treated to a memorable display of black humour. Fellow crew members John Gibson and Andrew Stevenson-Hamilton performed a mock execution. Wearing dark glasses

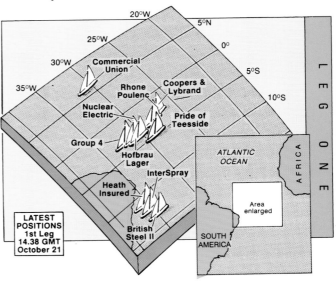

and a balaclava marked "Tactician", Gibson emerged through the companionway tapping a white stick, leading Hamilton out

The sail of the century.

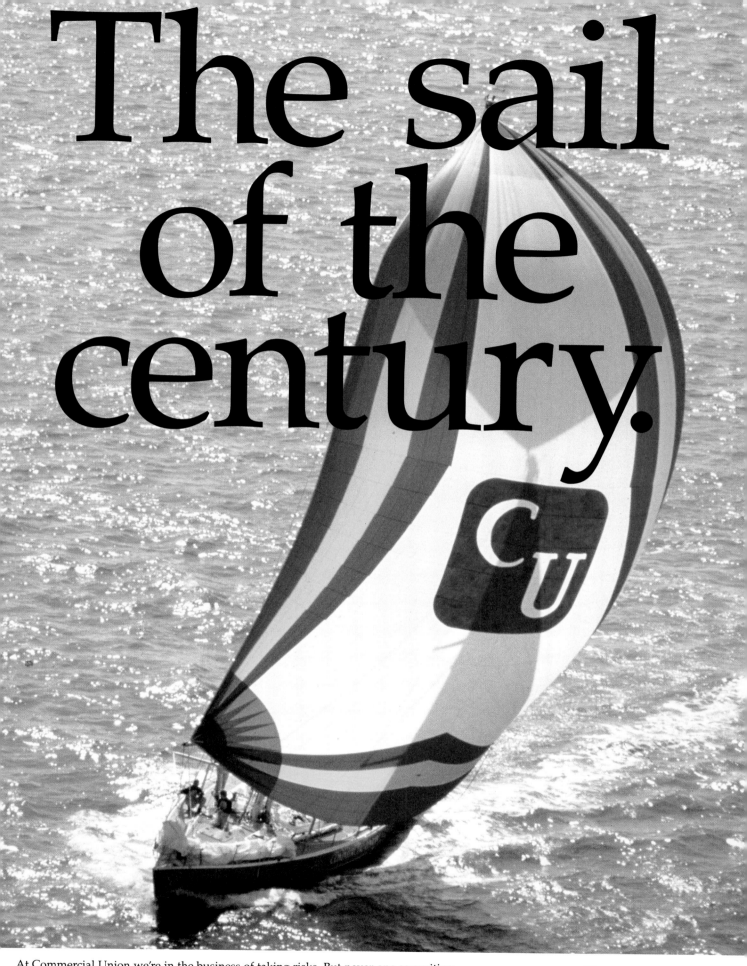

At Commercial Union we're in the business of taking risks. But never one so exciting
...e British Steel Challenge.

To take on the oceans of the world is a tremendous achievement for every crew.

Not least our own, who arrived home safely and a worthy second, in the final dash
...Capetown.

It's good to have them back. And great to have been part of the adventure.

COMMERCIAL UNION

We won't make a drama out of a crisis.

with a bag over his head inscribed "Navigator" and a noose round his neck!

Once ashore, some of the crew poured out their feelings. Jonathan Norton, a 24-year-old insurance broker from London,

Just rewards: Infolink winner Richard Tudor, skipper of British Steel II, receives his prize from Chay Blyth in the shadow of the Sugarloaf

said: "Will is a nice enough man, but he has no skills as a manager. We just lost faith in his leadership and ability to take us down into the Southern Ocean on the next leg."

Alison McKichan, a freelance market researcher from Edinburgh, was equally critical. "If anything, I feel sorry for him. But he had such a demoralising effect on us. Any time we were having fun, he would put the dampeners on it."

"The start was a shambles. We all had families there and were very embarrassed. It was our big chance, and to have such a complete disaster was humiliating. From there on it just went from bad to worse."

Sutherland argued with Blyth that matters could still be talked through as they had been in Southampton, but the die had been cast. A replacement skipper, Richard Merriweather, had already been flown out to take over. At 27 he was the youngest skipper in the race, but his track record appeared to make him ideal for the task. Apart from his six transatlantic crossings and a racing pedigree gained aboard such well known yachts as Highland Fling, he had spent the past year taking underprivileged and difficult kids from Britain's inner cities to sea on a sail training yacht. He seemed just the man, we thought, for this strong-willed bunch.

Commercial Union, the yacht sponsor, kept its promise not to make a drama out of a crisis, by saying as little as possible. Kate Whittaker, a spokesperson for the company which had adopted the unfortunate race slogan "We're behind you all the way", said: "We knew what was going to happen, but were not able to tell anyone" before dropping her guard and adding: "And yes, we would all like to shoot the copywriter who came

up with that advertising line!"

With the small matter of a mutiny now resolved, Chay Blyth was left to resolve the thorny issue of weather faxes, or rather the lack of them during this first leg. The equipment failures had angered sponsors so much that some had called on their lawyers to see if the results could be nullified. Once all the yachts were in port, however, it transpired that the computers had worked fitfully, or not at all, on all but the ninth-placed Coopers & Lybrand. Blyth argued successfully that these breakdowns had made little or no difference to the results.

One sponsor continued to mutter darkly of conspiracies, but Blyth fended off further problems from that quarter by getting each skipper to sign a joint statement agreeing that if any one of them was unhappy with new equipment installed on the yachts in Rio, then it would be removed from all yachts before the start and crews would have to rely on weather information telexed directly from race control in Petersfield.

"This is a test of human initiative. Dealing with equipment, functioning or not, is an integral part of the Challenge. It is unfortunate that this equipment has not lived up to expectations, but we will be replacing it all before the next leg," Blyth assured everyone.

It was a hot issue at Rio but, with icebergs waiting for the fleet off the River Plate, and freezing spray in the Roaring Forties, further complaints were soon lost on the wind, once the fleet set sail for Cape Horn and Tasmania.

"Cape Horn to Starboard"

Down Into
the Unknown

Samba-vibrating Rio is a place to love or hate. There are no half measures. The sun-bleached sands of Copacabana, stunningly beautiful women, the palm-skirted Sugarloaf mountain and the famous statue of Christ the Redeemer stand in direct contrast to the muggings, drugs, vice and the humidity.

Mike Martin and Carol McBean will for ever have fond memories of the place. Despite the best efforts of the British Steel team to sidetrack their crew mate during a riotous stag-night in the downtown red-light district, the pair managed to tie the knot in a marriage ceremony conducted by a Rio judge aboard the yacht. The couple then escaped for a few days to a mountain retreat, leaving others to argue in the oppressive heat about spinnakers, electronic gizmos and skippers, and worry themselves silly about the Southern Ocean.

Two days after mutiny forced Will Sutherland to step off Commercial Union, David Johnson, one of Blyth's amateur recruits aboard Nuclear Electric, threw in the towel. The 56-year-old business studies teacher from Eastbourne decided that he was not fit enough to take on Cape Horn or the Roaring Forties, but hoped to rejoin the race for the final leg back up the Atlantic from Cape Town. "During this first stage, I found that my movement, my ability to walk around the yacht, was badly impaired in rough conditions," he explained. "It made me feel physically exhausted and I couldn't pull my weight. I fell twice one night in relatively calm conditions. I'm not in my first flush of youth and all this distracts from the general enjoyment of the race. I have sailed for 20 years and don't want to lose my love of the sport."

Skipper John Chittenden and Blyth both called it "a brave decision". "It's tough for a man who has given up his job and house to take on this challenge and then admit that he cannot continue," said Blyth. "It says a lot about him, because it must have been very difficult to accept."

Johnson's place on Nuclear Electric was taken by Martin Barker, a 31-year-old mechanical craftsman from Heysham 2 power station. Initially, he thought his call up was to fix the yacht's engine, just as he had done when Nuclear Electric had visited his home port. "I was absolutely gob-smacked when I realised I was actually being asked to join the crew," he said after being told he would be heading on for Cape Horn and the rigours of the Southern Ocean.

Ken Ellis, another amateur, this time from Hofbräu Lager,

also chose to fly home after sickness and back trouble made a misery of his first leg. "I hugely enjoyed competing on the first stage from Southampton - it's been one of the greatest experiences of my life. But I had to consider my crew. I felt I could handle the sea sickness, but my back complaint made the rest of the voyage an unrealistic risk," reasoned the 52-year-old fish farmer from Merseyside.

The game of musical chairs continued on the professional side too. Just a week before the restart John O'Driscoll, Rhône-Poulenc's skipper, also decided that he could not continue. It became apparent soon after the yacht had finished eighth in Rio that the 55-year-old Royal Navy diver, who had been a last-minute replacement for Alec Honey, had not enjoyed the experience. Most of the crew did not get a chance to sail with him before the start and, quite apart from the inevitable clashes of personality that developed on board, he found it hard to get them to do things his way. They had also spent the past six months training under the guidance of Whitbread Round the World Race-winner Lionel Pean. The Frenchman's presence in Rio during the stopover merely added to the friction, and O'Driscoll's withdrawal came as no surprise.

To misplace one skipper was unfortunate. To lose two began to look like carelessness. The loss of three so early in the Challenge was music to the ears of the many cynics back home.

Blyth faced the criticisms head on. "We would have preferred to have had ten skippers start and the same ten finish. It is our mistake as organisers if things go wrong in this area. Perhaps we should have had them all in place earlier," he said after calling on Peter Phillips, an old rival from his multihull-racing days, to restore credibility.

Phillips, a 56-year-old former police sergeant from Exeter with a reputation for blunt, candid one-liners, was in place within 48 hours to give himself six days to "knock this demoralised crew into shape".

His arrival hit the boat like a tornado. "I'm going all the way round. If anyone gets off at Hobart or Cape Town it won't be me," he barked, adding: "This first leg has been a walk in the sun. Now they are about to learn that this is not a nice game. There is talk of seasickness on board. It doesn't matter. So long as we have nine bodies on deck, we can win."

Simon Walker, the first mate aboard Rhône-Poulenc said: "We are sorry to see John go, but we have a strong crew that is deeply committed to working together and are looking forward to creating a winning team with Peter." It didn't quite materialise that way, but the hard-drinking policeman and his crew certainly livened up the stopovers.

Away from the safety of the plush Rio Yacht Club, some sailors ran into all sorts of trouble. Yvonne Flatman, a watch leader on British Steel, was mugged at knife-point during an evening stroll along Copacabana beach. She returned to the hotel without her watch and considerably wiser. A race official also had his money stolen by a pickpocket.

Another victim was Bill Vincent who had money, credit cards and every stitch of clothing taken from his hotel room while he slept. The first anyone knew of his problems was when a sheepish looking Heath crewman was spotted riding naked down in the lift to call on a crew mate to lend him some clothes.

The high humidity and tummy troubles that worked progressively through the fleet did little to keep heads cool. Arguments were allowed to ferment, then invariably blew up like grenades - often in Blyth's face.

The first complaint lobbed his way was an extra GPS position repeater fitted in the cockpit of British Steel II. The instrument gave the helmsman a visual display of navigation information, available only at the chart table below decks on rival yachts. Other skippers felt aggrieved and disadvantaged, and demanded the £1,000 instrument be fitted on their yachts. "If I had found out about this earlier in the leg, I would have considered a protest," said Heath Insured's skipper Adrian Donovan.

Tudor, however, had followed all the rules. He had gained written permission from the race management before fitting the equipment which he said "provided no tactical advantage. The repeater simply saved you the chore of going below for information".

Such was the furore that Blyth and his team were forced to change their ruling. "There was a perception among the fleet that it gave British Steel II an advantage, so we had to react to that, even if it wasn't technically an accurate complaint," Blyth told The Times, adding: "It was also a business decision. All the boats wanted one and we weren't about to spend that kind of money."

More controversy was stirred up over the question of penalties for spinnakers ripped beyond repair during the first leg. Michael Calvin, the Daily Telegraph's chief sports writer who built up a large following for his perceptive reports from on board Hofbräu Lager, voiced the concerns of many whose prudence over sail care had cost them valuable time. "If the race committee decide to allow yachts to replace damaged spinnakers without penalty, this appears to contradict the founding principal of the race, which insists good seamanship should be rewarded," he wrote.

The problem for Blyth was that the blown spinnakers, such as those on Heath Insured and Rhône-Poulenc, had all ripped around their logos, suggesting that the paint had weakened the material. In the end, Blyth side-stepped the issue by removing all the branded sails and replacing them with asymmetric

spinnakers which, it was thought, would be easier to control in strong winds.

After four weeks in Rio, the old adage "ports rot men and ships" began to turn into reality and, despite worries about the unknown, almost all of Blyth's recruits were itching to get started for Cape Horn. For these 140 adventurers, which included 19 new recruits, The Cape was seen as the most daunting stage of the next 8,850-mile voyage to Hobart, Tasmania.

At the infamous Cape, they had read, the winds are gale force most days and stormy the rest, building up to hurricane force for three or four days each month. After that, they would meet the full force of the low pressure systems sweeping eastward around the Roaring Forties and Furious Fifties.

There was also the ever-present threat of running into an

Bone in her teeth: Coopers & Lybrand enjoys a lively start from Rio, en route to Cape Horn. No quarter was asked for, or given as the crews jostled for position

iceberg or the growlers that break off the main berg and lie unseen, semi-submerged beneath the waves.

Blyth reinforced the potential dangers ahead by reciting an extract from that sailor's bible, the Admiralty pilot book "Ocean Passages of The World" during his final crew briefing: "Icebergs are most numerous SE of the Cape of Good Hope and midway between Kerguelen Island and the meridian of Cape Leeuwin. The periods of frequency vary greatly. It may happen that while ships are passing ice in lower latitudes, others in higher latitudes find the ocean free of it. The lengths of many of the Southern Ocean icebergs are remarkable. Bergs of 5-20 miles in length are frequently sighted S of the 40th parallel, and bergs of 20-50 miles in length are far from uncommon."

"It may be gathered from numerous observations that bergs may be found anywhere S of the 30th parallel, that as many as 4,500 bergs have been observed in a run of 2,000 miles, that estimated heights of from 240-520 metres are not uncommon, and that bergs of from 60-82 miles in length are numerous."

> *"This next stage will not be a delivery trip. The Southern Ocean is hostile and nobody goes there for pleasure."*

It was all daunting stuff to anyone whose most terrifying experience of ice had been on a black run during a skiing holiday in Kitzbuehl...

Adrian Rayson, the Heath Insured crewman, was among those trying to suppress these fears as his crew cast off the ropes and headed for the start line off Copacabana. "The first leg was a glorious off-wind sail down the Atlantic. For many of us, it was our first experience of true 'blue-water' racing. The pitfalls that could arise now will stem from the euphoria of completing this first stage. Ken Pearson, our watch leader, has warned us that there is no room for complacency. This next stage will not be a delivery trip. The Southern Ocean is hostile and nobody goes there for pleasure," he wrote in his log.

Apart from Blyth, only two competitors had been down there before and both were aboard Nuclear Electric. John Chittenden, her skipper, had led Creighton's Naturally when she had run this gauntlet from the opposite direction during the previous Whitbread race. His watch leader, Steve Yates, had completed two circumnavigations on the same boat.

"It will be interesting to see how my crew fares," Chittenden reflected. "The intense cold could have a serious effect on morale. I went down as far as 62 degrees South during the Whitbread race, but we are unlikely to go much further than 58 degrees on this leg because we have to round a navigational way-point that stops us diving deep into iceberg territory and following the shortest route."

To combat the cold, crews were equipped with the latest thermal and protective clothing. "We've no trouble keeping

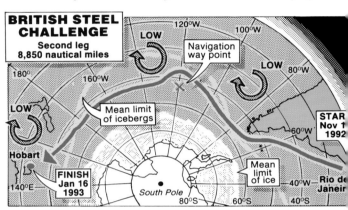

warm. We have everything from survival suits to gloves and goggles," said Chittenden. "The problem will be drying it all out between watches."

At the time, the weather maps suggested that these crews might find the stage easier than anyone expected. The clockwise-spinning low pressures systems that usually circle the pack-ice in the Screaming Sixties had been pushed well north of the race course and even of Cape Horn, offering the unusual prospect of reaching and running winds for much of the leg. Everybody

They're off again: the re-start from Rio took place under blazing skies, with a fresh breeze. There were several incidents, including a collision involving Heath Insured (top right) and Nuclear Electric. The former was obliged to turn back and round the outer distance mark before resuming course

HOFBRÄU
MÜNCHEN

Munich is at the very heart of Bavarian brewing tradition. Munich. A city of castles and palaces. Of gardens and galleries. And at its centre - The Hofbräuhaus Court Brewery.

The Hofbräuhaus was founded in 1589 by the Royal Duke of Bavaria Wilhelm V. His ancestors created the Reinheitsgebot, The German Purity Law, for beer brewing.

It remained in the family ownership until 1919, when taken over by the State it became something of a national treasure. Today, after four hundred years, the Hofbräuhaus is still at the heart of Munich's way of life. As is the beer which bears its famous name. Hofbräu.

Only available in the UK through: Hall & Woodhouse Ltd, The Brewery, Blandford St. Mary, Dorset. DT11 9LS Tel: 0258 452141

The Hofbräuhaus courtyard in Munich 1859.

knew, however, that the headwinds promised in Blyth's brochure could turn this adventure into misery. With ambient temperatures hovering at freezing point, the wind chill factor would reduce temperatures on deck down to -15 degrees.

"Morale will be at its lowest ebb about a month out, so I am breaking this stage into three legs. We will be having a party at Cape Horn and another at the International Dateline," said Chittenden, adding prophetically: "And a very big one in Hobart!"

Icebergs were again high on the agenda on the eve of the start. One the size of the Isle of Wight had reportedly grounded off the river Plate and split into fragments, two of which were

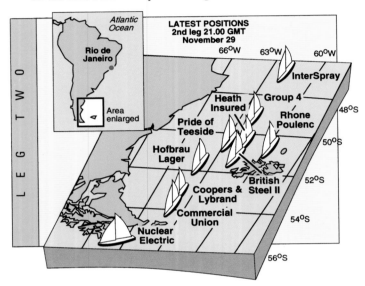

known to be more than 100ft high. Peter Phillips, who had spent the previous day coaching his crew in the art of tacking and gybing - in between the spans of the 13 mile-long Rio-Niteroi road bridge while other teams relaxed in pool-side bars - was delighted by the news. "It will give us a chance to see one of nature's most spectacular sights before we hit the Southern Ocean," he exclaimed.

The fleet set out for Cape Horn in dramatic fashion on 15 November, breasting steep seas and 20-knot winds. Pete Goss, skipper of Hofbräu Lager, judged the line to perfection, forcing InterSpray over the line seconds ahead of time. Luckily for Paul Jeffes the Rio race committee failed to recall his yacht correctly, and InterSpray led the fleet away without incurring a penalty for failing to recross.

There was further drama at the favoured weather end of the line when John Chittenden's Nuclear Electric edged Group 4 and Heath Insured the wrong side of the mark. Chittenden was in the right but his yacht carried the scars of her collision with Donovan's yacht all the way to Hobart. "This is amazing. They have 8,800 miles ahead of them, yet they are not giving each other an inch. These guys have lost their innocence since the start from Southampton," said an excited Blyth from a hill-top overlooking the bay.

At the Fairway buoy directly off Copacabana Beach there was little more than shouts and spray dividing them as InterSpray led British Steel II, Hofbräu, Teesside and Nuclear

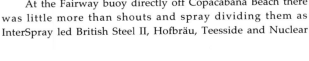

"A few 'pavement pizzas' still appearing on the leeward rail, but morale is high."

Electric round. They were followed in short order by Coopers & Lybrand, CU Assurance, Rhône-Poulenc and Group 4 with the Heath crew bringing up the rear, protest flag fluttering hopefully in their rigging.

Crews may have struggled to gain their sea-legs, but the racing continued at a furious pace with the lead changing four times within the first two days. "A few 'pavement pizzas' still appearing on the leeward rail, but morale is high," reported a cheerful Adrian Rayson as Heath Insured fought to overhaul Mike Golding's men on Group 4 Securitas.

The two crews were still within sight of each other, four days after the start, when the bottle-screw holding Group 4's forestay snapped at 0300 GMT as the yacht was beating into a 30-knot breeze. This brought consternation to her crew who had, by now, worked their way up to fifth. Luckily, the mast stayed in one piece and no one was injured, but the stay, swinging violently around the foredeck, badly lacerated the headsail before the crew could get hold of it. "We fell off a couple of waves with a sickening crash and mayhem broke out," Golding reported. "Mike O'Regan and Simon Littlejohn attached two spinnaker halyards to act as a temporary forestay, but it took five men to lash down the forestay and sail."

As the crew set a fresh course towards Florianopolis under main and staysail, Group 4's headquarters in Worcestershire went into overdrive, collecting the spare parts from Southampton and Nottingham and flying them out to Brazil in time for the yacht to rejoin the race within 48 hours.

They did it majestically, throwing in a chartered Lear jet, for good measure, to get Nick Jubert and John Carter back from Sao Paulo with the repaired headsail after the pair missed the commercial flight back to Florianopolis.

The diversion cost the crew 250 miles on Nuclear Electric, which by now had built up a commanding 120-mile lead over the fleet after taking an extreme easterly course down the South American coast. But Group 4 also had the wind close inshore, and while yachts like InterSpray and British Steel II found themselves all but becalmed, Golding and his men were speeding south at 11 knots, almost six knots faster than these tail-enders.

By 24 November, nine days into the leg, Chittenden's crew had extended their lead to almost 240 miles after pulling a further 96 miles ahead of second-placed yacht Commercial Union overnight. However, it was the sight of a berg, floating unseasonably high at 42 degrees South, that had everyone talking within the fleet. "We have waited over a week for ice to go with the gin and tonics," Nuclear Electric's skipper quipped before going on to describe the 250ft-high and half-mile wide iceberg found floating 360 miles off the Argentine coast. "It's comparable in size to the Thames Barrier," he said.

By now, Heath Insured had moved out to follow Nuclear Electric's easterly course and was the second most southerly yacht within the fleet, though still lying sixth in terms of distance to Cape Horn. The battle for second place was being hotly contested by four yachts, Rhône-Poulenc, Coopers & Lybrand, Hofbräu Lager and Commercial Union, whose crew swept up from ninth to fourth during the previous night following a 48-hour charge of 332 miles. They were spread out almost line abreast between 180 and 360 miles off the Argentine coast, but in terms of distance to Cape Horn, 16 miles was all that divided them.

"The Chittendales", as Nuclear Electric's crew were called

THE CHALLENGE ROUND THE WORLD YACHT RACE

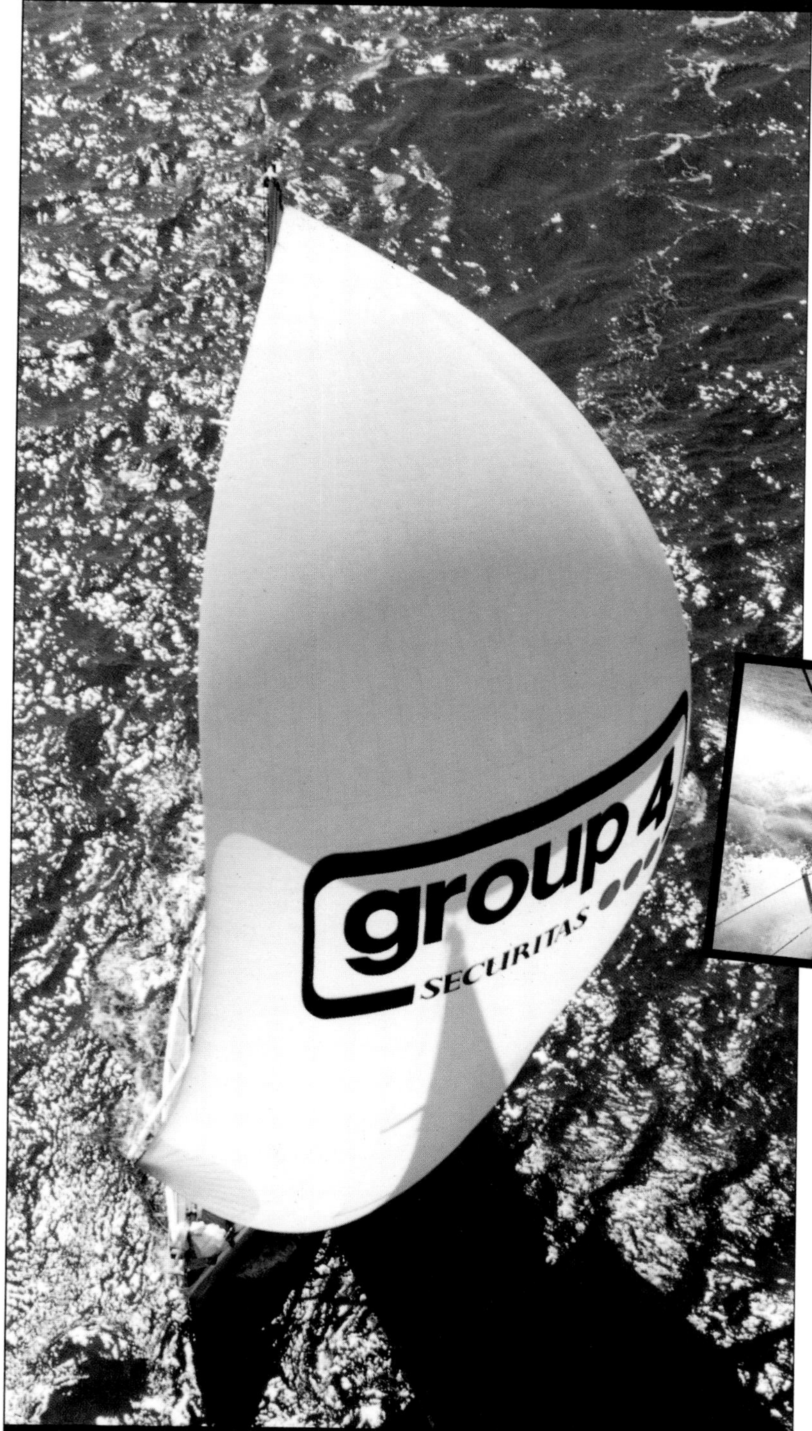

group 4
SECURITAS

Our heartfelt congratulations go to skipper Mike Golding and the Group 4 crew. Their historic achievement, finishing only 1 hour 10 minutes behind the winning yacht after 28,000 miles of sailing in the British Steel Challenge Round-the-World Yacht Race, proves once again that the Group 4 name is synonymous with teamwork, courage and a determination to rise above all setbacks.

For in the nine months they have been away, the Group 4 crew have, like ourselves, found that being the best in the world can sometimes be anything but plain sailing.

On 17th November 1992, for instance, a vital part of their mast was damaged beyond repair in high seas and 30 knots of wind off the coast of South America. Yet, thanks to the numerous Group 4 services which sourced and delivered identical replacement parts within a matter of hours, even a problem of this magnitude could not weaken their resolve or resilience.

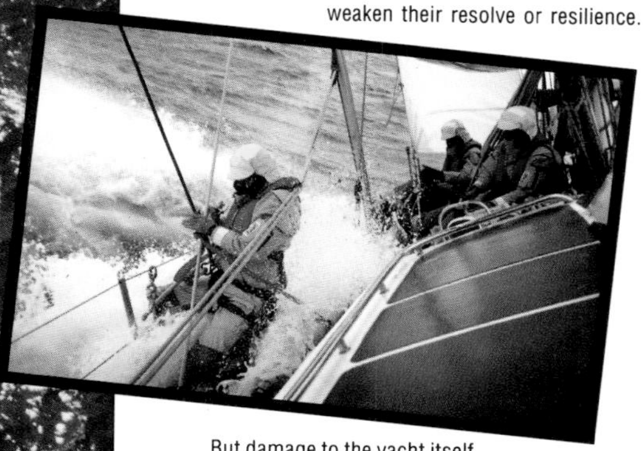

But damage to the yacht itself wasn't all the crew had to face, with broken ribs, damaged knees and a whole host of cuts and bruises also being encountered and overcome. At the end of the day, however, each and every knock made them all the more determined to succeed.

Wherever our name appears, you can be certain that the same dedication prevails, and that throughout our many unrivalled services, training and professionalism will ensure that Group 4, like its yacht, is always a match for the competition.

WINNERS TO CAPE TOWN WINNERS TO SOUTHAMPTON
SECOND OVERALL

group 4 SECURITAS

Group 4 Limited,
Farncombe House, Broadway, Worcestershire WR12 7LJ
Telephone:0386 858585 Fax: 0386 852861

PROFESSIONALISM IN THE FACE OF ADVERSITY

Below: icebergs were predicted to be one of the greatest hazards of the leg, and a careful radar watch was needed. This berg, however, was spotted by the crew of Nuclear Electric off the mouth of the River Plate. Right: the on-watch crew of Pride of Teesside huddle on the side decks, in typical cold weather

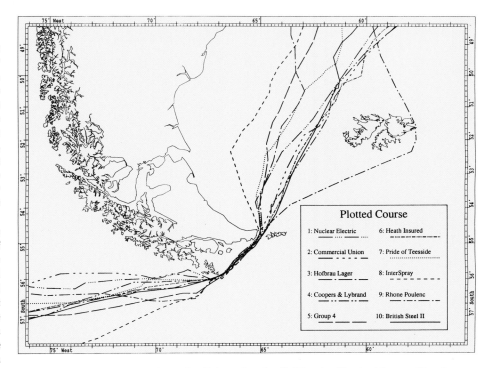

Plotted Course

1: Nuclear Electric   6: Heath Insured

2: Commercial Union   7: Pride of Teesside

3: Hofbrau Lager   8: InterSpray

4: Coopers & Lybrand   9: Rhone Poulenc

5: Group 4   10: British Steel II

in recognition of their unique cabaret act ashore, rounded Cape Horn shortly before 2000 GMT on 29 November, having fought an almost unequal battle against the weather during the previous 24 hours when they had been able to make little more than three knots into the teeth of a 30-knot sou'wester. Then, just as they were within sight of the Horn, the capricious wind died to less than five knots, leaving the crew slopping uncomfortably around in 6ft swells.

"I have 598 weather observations for the Horn on my chart and just two of them indicate calms. It's all very frustrating. Wherever we go the wind seems to head us. We spent several hours on Saturday almost becalmed just north of the Strait de le Maire and have met headwinds ever since," Chittenden told us when we went out from Cape Horn to greet the crew aboard a Chilean Navy supply ship.

As if on cue to mark Nuclear Electric's arrival, the clouds suddenly rolled away and the sun sent temperatures soaring above 20 degrees. "It's never like this here," said Lieutenant Alberto Alterman, commanding our small ship. "You are very lucky to see the Horn in these conditions."

Chittenden and his crew didn't quite see it the same way, but consoled themselves by sharing out the contents of a bottle of Scotch secreted on board by one unnamed crewman. "We're also looking forward to eating some pasties cooked by Richard Rollinshaw, our baker from Brighton," Chittenden shouted across before adding darkly: "He also cooked some sausages this morning and someone has pinched five that were left in the pan. We will have to have an enquiry about that!"

Despite attempts at a Mexican wave for the TV camera, their disappointment at finding the Horn in such a passive mood was clear. They had spent every spare moment during the past week reading the many horrific tales from the great days of sail and had wanted a fight to remember.

The worst year this century was 1905 when more than 400 square-riggers made, or attempted to make, voyages round Cape Horn. At least six ships disappeared without trace. Many more were wrecked, driven aground on the tooth-like rocks

Hofbräu Lager takes an icy ducking

around the island, or suffered so much damage at the hands of the wind and sea that they were deemed total losses when eventually they limped into port. At least 40 were forced to turn

and run in distress for the Falklands, Montevideo or Rio. A dozen more gave up the battle and ran right round the world before the Roaring Forties' gales in order to reach their destinations from the other side of the globe.

So Chittenden's crew, now 143 miles ahead of second-placed Commercial Union Assurance, got off lightly, as did the rest of the fleet, for the conditions remained balmy almost continuously for a record seven days. "We have never known it like this before," admitted the lighthouse keeper. "Normally it rains every day!"

If the crew on Nuclear Electric were having an easy time, those on Rhône-Poulenc and InterSpray, bringing up the rear 500 miles or so astern, were not. Peter Phillips reported over the radio that they had fallen victim to a vicious 40-knot blast of Pampero which had knocked Rhône-Poulenc on her beam-ends and damaged her rigging. The yacht was now heading for Port Stanley in the Falklands to make repairs. Meanwhile John Davis, a watch leader on InterSpray, was laid up in his bunk nursing a sore head after the spinnaker pole had accidentally crashed down on him.

Richard Merriweather's crew rounded the Horn in second place amid a flock of sea birds a day after The Chittendales. It was a performance in stark contrast to CU's torrid first leg voyage to Rio. Crewman Andrew Stevenson-Hamilton had nothing but praise for their new skipper. "Richard has transformed the skills and attitudes on board. There is a new positive feeling on CU. There is still room for improvement, and changes aimed at increasing boat speed were made even before leaving Rio. These include a change in watch system with each crew given a designated position on the yacht. Much work is being done to improve strategy with three or four of us involved in the daily decisions. Above all, we now work together as a team. Racing has become physically exhausting because our new approach demands much more from us, but we are prepared to give our all."

Vince Hughes, who had joined the yacht at Rio and had been one of biggest dissenters of Will Sutherland's tenure during the months of training, took the opportunity to exorcise the boat

Rounding the Horn: Rhône-Poulenc finds the Cape in benign mood

Traditional Horners' ear-piercing as Teesside crew puts his head on the block

The first sign of trouble to come. Group 4's bottle-screw

Teesside celebrate rounding the Horn

of all memories of their previous skipper by performing a "burial service" with a wooden plaque bearing Sutherland's name, presented in his absence at Rio. "After that piece of black humour, Will became something of a taboo subject on board," admitted Merriweather.

The Cape finally lost its charm the following day when a depression swept in from the Southern Ocean, bringing with it a force-ten storm and rain squalls. These were more like the conditions for which most crews had conditioned themselves, but with the winds swinging round to the north-west, the waters remained remarkably smooth - in the shadows of Cape Horn at least.

> "We have never known it like this before," admitted the lighthouse keeper. "Normally it rains every day!"

Vivien Cherry's team on Coopers & Lybrand were cheated of the sight by pitch darkness but the crew were pleased to be in third place. She told us over the radio as they passed our lighthouse home: "All we can see is a dark lump in the night, but we have held up a white door and photographed the words 'Cape Horn' for posterity."

They were followed later that day first by Hofbräu Lager, then British Steel II whose crew had made a remarkable fight-back from the rear of the fleet. Two of the crew, Yvonne Flatman and David Arthur, had been laid up in their bunks by lengthy bouts of food poisoning picked up in Rio.

Later in the day, Pride of Teesside and Heath Insured rounded within five minutes of each other. Their match-race antics, which continued throughout this leg, coincided with a flight over the Horn by the local Chilean Naval commander checking one of his most southern outposts. He could not believe his eyes. There, standing naked at the wheel of Heath reading what looked like a newspaper, was a man. "You English are mad. Who else would sail down here like

that," said the flabbergasted commander after his helicopter landed by our lighthouse.

"It's a lie," retorted Heath crewman Adrian Rayson with mock indignation when we questioned the yacht over the radio. "He was not naked. David Spratley was wearing a bobble hat, and he was holding a sign, not a newspaper" he added.

It was a pity about the bobble hat. Without it, Spratley could well have claimed to have been the first known nude yachtsman to have shot the Horn. Instead he at least has a photographic memento of the sign he held up, which reads: "[arrow left] Cape of Good Hope. Cape Horn [arrow right] Hopeless Horn [arrow downwards]."

Group 4 went round in the dead of night, her crew disappointed at not seeing the Horn, but elated that they had already picked off two of the fleet. They also had their hands full. "We've just topped 18 knots surfing down a wave. It's exhilarating out here," Golding reported over the radio to us as the wind indicator at our lighthouse hovered for a short period on 50 knots.

We waited another day for InterSpray, then waited a further 16 hours to see the back of them as the calms that had beset Jeffes and his crew almost from the first week out of Rio continued to plague their progress.

Behind them, Peter Phillips and his crew on Rhône-Poulenc had been halted, not by calms, but by the social life within Port Stanley. "We just couldn't get rid of them," laughed the wireless operator from HMS Dumbarton Castle when we met him on our return to Punta Arenas where he was taking leave from his ship.

"We helped them all we could, repairing and re-rigging their mast, but the crew just wouldn't leave until they had drunk our ship dry. Now we intend to do the same to them when they return to Southampton," he laughed.

Phillips and his crew had the most enjoyable rounding on 4 December, a day behind InterSpray, despite the antics of our helicopter pilot who doused them with his downwash. With the winds blowing a fulsome 25 knots on a bright sunny day, 58-year-old Campbell MacKenzie found himself overawed by the sight of the Horn. "It is like standing on Everest," he said. His son Angus, a stowaway from Rio, was less philosophical but just as impressed. "It's like going to a party where there is only one attractive girl - and she is talking to me!," he laughed.

On 6 December, news from Vivien Cherry sent chill shudders through the race organisation sitting in the centrally-heated comfort of their Petersfield headquarters. The forestay bottle-screw on Coopers & Lybrand had parted in exactly the same way as the one on Group 4 two weeks earlier. Thanks to fast reactions on the part of Robert Faulds at the wheel and the immense strength of the mast, the rig had stayed up. "It resulted in a brain-storming session as we were 1,000 miles from land," reported Cherry. "Various options were considered before we decided to replace the broken bottle-screw with another holding

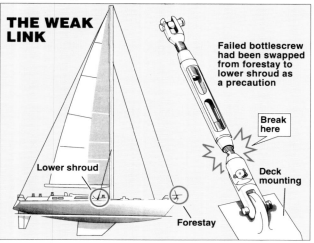

THE WEAK LINK

Failed bottlescrew had been swapped from forestay to lower shroud as a precaution

Break here

Lower shroud

Deck mounting

Forestay

a side stay. Until it was complete, we didn't think it was possible to effect a 100 per cent repair, and surprised ourselves and the fleet by our speedy repair," she said proudly after handing celebratory beers out all round.

But worse was to come. Within hours, Mike Golding was telexing back to Race HQ that Group 4 had experienced a repeat of their earlier forestay failure less than 2,000 miles after fitting a replacement. This knocked down the initial theory that simple fatigue was the cause. Mercifully, the rig did not collapse and no one was injured.

With the failure now of three forestay bottle-screws on identical yachts, many began to ask the fateful question. Was there a time-bomb ticking away?

Pete Goss had skippered the prototype training yacht British Steel Challenge for much of the previous year. The boat had never experienced any failure like this - even when hitting the span of a bridge in Stavanger, Norway (when the forestay rather than bottle-screws parted). This latest damaged left Goss totally perplexed. "It amazes me that they are giving out when you consider I had the same fitting on the prototype for a very hard 28,000 miles in much harsher conditions than we are experiencing now, when we went from the extremes of -30 degrees C to force 12 winds. One thing the problem does underline is that the boats are fantastic. To think that one rig has lost its forestay twice while powering to windward and is still standing, is very reassuring. We have a safe platform."

On 9 December, 25 days after leaving Rio, Chittenden's crew passed the halfway point to Hobart. The Commercial Union crew, however, was chasing hard, having closed the gap down to a tenuous 66 miles. Another to move up was British Steel II, now in third place. "Morale is high, but it is very cold," reported Louise Broadbent, the youngest crew member on board. "The seas are getting rough. We are all wearing many layers of clothing and doing our shifts on deck with no skin exposed at all. Steering is exhilarating with such huge waves and frequent squalls, and moving around is very difficult with the yacht on its side and bouncing off the big waves."

Those in the middle of the Southern Ocean were not the only ones to be white faced. The first satellite telex bills were landing on sponsors' desks, and they looked more like the national debt of some banana republic. The Heath Group fired off an immediate order calling on their crew to restrict messages to a minimum - which Adrian Rayson did by cutting out all vowels in the next press report sent back to their London headquarters. It took the poor insurance men a day to translate and, at the end of it, a counter-command was sent back to the boat - typed in full!

On 12 December, Nuclear Electric was first to round the navigational waypoint set at 52 degrees South, 120 degrees West to keep crews from diving too far south on the shortest, most dangerous course around the bottom of the globe. Ironically, the point that Blyth and his team had picked with a pin on their chart was unusually surrounded by icebergs - the very dangers the yachts had been diverted northwards to avoid. Chittenden's men sighted two the previous day and gave their positions to the rest of the fleet, but they now had Commercial Union Assurance within 37 miles of them.

Within 24 hours, six more crews had followed round, three of them within sight of each other - a stunning endorsement for one-design racing. Goss reported: "Rounding the waypoint was charged with excitement because Heath Insured

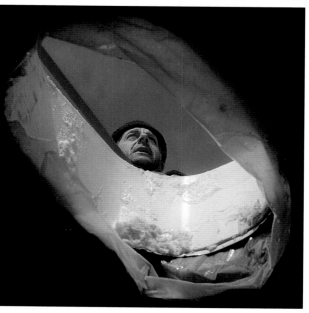

Devestation: the end of a dream as British Steel's crew face up to the fact that their chances of victory are over. "What we want is for Father Christmas to drop a new mast down the hole in our deck," says Kevin Dufficy. After they were helped with extra supplies of fuel from Group 4 and Heath Insured, the P&O container ship New Zealand Pacific diverted to drop off a further 1,000 litres of diesel

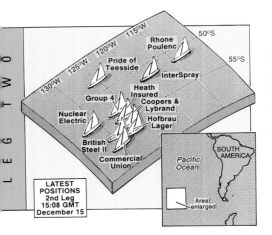

LATEST
POSITIONS
2nd Leg
15:08 GMT
December 15

suddenly came into sight to leeward of us seven miles out. Excitement then changed to elation when we heard over the radio that Pride of Teesside, though out of sight from us, could see Heath too."

Aboard Adrian Donovan's Heath Insured, however, all was not well. The forestay bottle-screw had just snapped, thankfully without leading to injury or damage. The crew swapped the broken bottom fork for another, robbed from a lower side shroud, but had to contend with several icebergs and avoid the attendant growlers as they ran off downwind to take the pressure off their damaged rig.

By now, tests on the first bottle-screw to break on Group 4 Securitas revealed that tensile overload, not fatigue, had caused the fitting to break. The report suggested that the sudden shock loads experienced by the yachts sailing through extreme conditions in freezing temperatures had created enormous pressures on the boats which sometimes exceeded the yield strength of the Norseman-Gibb fitting.

These problems did nothing to dampen Richard Merriweather's drive to the front of the fleet. His Commercial Union crew finally wore down Nuclear Electric's lead on 14 December after ducking 200 miles further south than Chittenden's men. For a short period that day Richard Tudor and his crew on British Steel II slipped ahead of Nuclear Electric before calamity struck them too.

Earlier in the day Tudor had given the outside world an idea of the conditions. "We are really feeling the Roaring Forties, experiencing 50-knot winds on the nose and huge seas. We are taking a pounding, but holding things together."

"Rounding Cape Horn we were lulled into a false sense of security! We are on edge while in iceberg territory. Maximum vigilance with a minimum of three crew on the freezing deck watching out and two on the radar below. Sleep is getting short with so much to do."

Two days later, his world came tumbling down around him

when British Steel II was suddenly dismasted - the result of yet another bottle-screw failure.

Crewman Kevin Dufficy described the scene. "A noise like a gunshot and this leg was over for us. A shout for all hands on deck; a roll call of the crew, relief that everyone was there, uninjured, and then the realisation that the sails were no longer there."

"The mast has broken, snapping like a twig at deck level, before disappearing into the Southern Ocean, dragging our sails and rigging with it. Fortunately, it did not put a hole in the yacht."

"Since the fourth day of this leg when Group 4 broke their forestay bottle-screw we have sailed well within ourselves. Then we were back in eighth place and have slowly worked our way up to second. For the past 36 hours we have weathered very strong gales with winds of 55 miles per hour and huge rolling seas - and the yacht was loving it. With just two small headsails set, she rode through the heavy seas comfortably. When the wind finally weakened to around 30 mph yesterday, we hoisted the mainsail part way up. Then the bottle-screw broke."

"There is a mood of quiet resignation on board. You have to accept events and get moving again. The crew have cleared up the debris and are now designing a makeshift mast and rigging so that we can get back into the race as soon as possible. The nearest land is New Zealand over 2,000 miles away. Any thoughts of spending New Year's Eve in Hobart, a realistic possibility given favourable winds, now lie 15,000 feet under the Southern Ocean at a spot marked on our chart at 56 degrees South 131 degrees West."

"We will still enjoy Christmas and New Year's Eve, as well as Marcus Gladwell's birthday, and we will follow the progress of the other yachts, wishing them a safe passage. But we wish Santa Claus could drop a mast down the hole in our deck. Getting to Hobart is important, but getting there faster than anyone else is the real challenge."

Pete Goss on Hofbräu was one of the first to offer assistance. "We are 77 miles from them and looking at our food stocks to see what we can spare," he telexed race HQ. Heath Insured and Group 4 Securitas, however, were first to reach the stricken yacht, arriving on the scene from different angles at almost exactly the same time. Working through the night, Group 4 went alongside first and passed 40 gallons of fuel across on ropes, and Tudor and his men received a further 65 gallons from Heath before passing back a CD of South Pacific as a 35th birthday present for Adrian Donovan.

Tudor reported: "The crew is tired. Everyone is working, grabbing a few hours sleep when absolutely necessary. But the jury rig is well on its way to completion. A boom and spinnaker pole act as our mast and rigging consists of a salvaged genoa, staysail sheets and reefing lines."

Meanwhile, Blyth's team was organising for the P&O container ship New Zealand Pacific, then berthed at Littleton, to take on 1,000 litres of fuel and divert from her course to Cape Horn to rendezvous with British Steel II.

Ian MacGillivray also offered to meet up with Tudor's crew and provide what assistance they could. His yacht, Pride of Teesside, had lost ground striking northwards the previous weekend for fear of running into icebergs after their radar appeared to pack up. They found out on the Monday that the set merely required re-initialising. After that, there was little more the fleet or race organisers could do.

Meanwhile, John Chittenden's more northerly course began

Christmas Day aboard Teesside: the weather outside was anything but cheerful as the crew made the most of their rations

to pay off and, on 18 December, Nuclear Electric regained a short lead over Commercial Union. Eight hundred miles astern the crew on Rhône-Poulenc, who also offered help to British Steel II if their courses coincided, were recovering from problems of their own after a huge wave had sent their boat into an involuntary tack four days before. Nick Fenner, who had been on the wheel when the wave swept down the deck, tried to turn the yacht back on her course but flailing ropes knocked him and fellow crewman Paul Egan over. Skipper Peter Phillips, who came out on deck to restore order, then helped the pair below. After looking at Egan's bruised face and cut lip, he reported back to Race HQ: "He looks very similar to a number of Friday night customers I used to deal with as a copper."

As Christmas Day dawned, fighting back the tears and pain of defrosting fingers in these icy wastes seemed a rather extreme way of avoiding the in-laws. The crew on the third-placed Hofbräu Lager had just hit a whale and, on a personal level, Jack Gordon Smith had cracked several ribs when thrown across the yacht by the wild seas. Fellow watch leader Tristan Lewis also suffered a dislocated shoulder as he tried to undress himself.

Meanwhile Geraint Lewis aboard Coopers & Lybrand was living on a cocktail of painkillers. He had been thrown out of his bunk and broke his collarbone. Fellow crewman Phil Jones had been suffering seasickness ever since stepping aboard the yacht six weeks before. "He's not going to feel any better until he is sitting safely under a tree in Hobart," skipper Vivien Cherry said.

> "He looks very similar to a number of Friday night customers I used to deal with as a copper."

The only yachts to avoid serious calamities within the ten-strong fleet were the front-runners. John Chittenden, a master mariner by trade, and perhaps the most experienced skipper, had been down here before and knew the fine line that divides derring-do from disaster. "We're racing one notch below maximum in these arduous conditions, working to avoid damage to the boat and crew," he told us. Richard Merriweather, at 27 the youngest skipper, with no previous experience of the Southern Ocean, was making sure that CU gave Nuclear Electric a run for its money. Their one problem on board had been rope burns suffered by Sue Tight.

Christmas was never far from anyone's mind. Much secrecy and advanced planning had surrounded preparations in Rio for the big day. Kate Twyman, on Pride of Teesside, for instance, had created stockings and crackers for her 13 crew mates while John Bagley had planned a lunch menu around McDougall's freeze-dried Chicken Supreme and boil-in-a-bag Christmas puddings.

Ken Pearson smuggled a Father Christmas suit aboard Heath Insured to wear when he served up the Dundee cake supplied by the sponsor's Scottish office and others had hidden the odd bottle in the bilges. Dave Spratley, who had already made the headlines for his naked antics at Cape Horn, was given a girlie calendar.

Cherry's crew went one further by not only having a tree in place, but dressing the yacht overall in fairy lights. "That was down to Barry Ford, our electrician," she told us, adding: "Alison Smith promises to be our fairy at the top of the mast." This all went to prove that the Christmas spirit can survive even the harshest environments.

For Tudor's crew on British Steel II, the best present of all

was the 1,000 litres of fuel transferred across from New Zealand Pacific on a bright Christmas morning. Two unwelcome gifts were broken bottle-screws experienced by Heath Insured and InterSpray during the festive period. After British Steel II's experience, everyone else was prepared, and rogue screws were quickly replaced.

Adrian Rayson reported from Heath: "There are balloons and streamers in the galley and cards curling with damp, but on deck the business of racing continues unabated. There are frustrations. The forestay failure and jury rig now makes reefing a cumbersome operation. One cannot relax, our minds are on the rig constantly; conservation the watchword. Headsails are changed earlier and reefs held in place longer than we prefer, but we have to sail over the finish line to stand a chance of winning. The spectre of British Steel II pervades."

By 27 December, Nuclear Electric had extended her lead over Commercial Union to 69 miles, but there was a price to pay. Crossing the International Dateline reduced Christmas to under 12 hours. One loser was Martin Baker who went to bed on

Peter Phillips makes a statement, whilst spreading his own brand of festive cheer aboard the yacht Rhône-Poulenc

Christmas Eve knowing he had the night watch off, and woke up 12 hours later to find it was Boxing Day.

Two days later, Heath Insured had their own story to tell when the yacht's steering cable broke as they crossed the "line". "The boat sailed herself across," Rayson told the world. "A cable parted and the wheel went round and round uselessly. If that was not enough, it was blowing old boots and we had the huge asymmetric spinnaker set."

The repair took two hours while Rayson used a stumpy emergency tiller to steer by. Then the wires parted again and it was another three hours before order was finally restored. Despite this damage, the team still managed a 24-hour run of 198 miles, losing just 34 miles to Pride of Teesside, the pace-setter that day. She had now pulled up to fourth - just ahead of Group 4 which the Teesside crew could see on the horizon.

Talking of this crossing of wakes, an amazed Mike Golding said: "After 7,000 miles, this was our first sighting of another yacht since breaking away from the fleet towards Florianopolis to repair our forestay. The whole crew came on deck as Teesside approached and crossed our stern about a mile away." The duel lasted two days before Golding decided to break away. "Racing in such close confines forces competitors to push their yachts to, and sometimes beyond, their limits," he said. "With our various jury rigs, pushing the yacht like this has been a restless time for me."

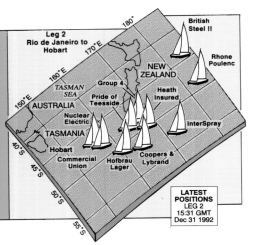

By now it was 1 January. The leading yachts were on converging courses within 500 miles of Hobart and promising another nail-biting finish. Nuclear Electric's lead over Commercial Union was 63 miles, but both crews knew that just one hiccough with the wind could reverse their roles.

Meanwhile, 1,000 miles to the west, British Steel II was tying up at Chatham Island. There they were to take on fuel and pick up a temporary mast, abandoned many years before when a boatbuilder's dream failed to come to fruition. The crew missed celebrating New Year's Eve thanks to a quirk in the Dateline which boxes this lonely Pacific outpost, but celebrated just the same in a pub near the quay.

The crew on Rhône-Poulenc, now trailing more than 1,000 miles behind the leaders, also lifted a glass or two that day. During the celebrations, they decided to play a practical joke on Chay Blyth. Turning the Commercial Union mutiny saga on its head, Peter Phillips fired off the following telex to his old rival over the yacht's satellite link:

TOP SECRET - FOR CHAY'S EYES ONLY

To: Chay Blyth
From: Peter Phillips
Date: 1 Jan 93

Dear Chay
We have a big problem on RP. It is New Year's Eve and I have instigated a very large party. As a result of that, the entire crew are drunk. At this time I can speak to you in complete confidence.

On arrival at Hobart, I will remain the skipper of RP. The same cannot be said of the crew. Will you please arrange for a complete replacement of 13 crew volunteers. Please treat this in complete confidence and do not release this until we have had a chance to discuss the outrageous and unsafe behaviour of the crew.

Although I did not pay for my berth, I feel entitled to make this decision as per the agreement with you before I left Rio.
A Happy New Year

Peter Phillips
PS. As crew know the INMARSAT system, please reply in code.

The effect was immediate and went beyond the hoaxers' wildest dreams. The message landed at Race HQ in the early hours of the morning and was read by a caretaker duty officer with orders not to disturb the management unless it was a matter of life and death. The officer, however, read it that way and passed it on to higher authority. Spencer Drummond, the race director, waited until daybreak to put an urgent call through to Helen Wybrow, the Challenge director responsible for crew matters.

She was just recovering from a heavy New Year's Eve party and the news hit her for six. This was the boat that had already had three skippers. What would the sponsors now say to this? With heart in mouth she raced back across Bodmin Moor to her office in North Cornwall to try and locate Chay, who by now was winging his way out to Hobart. It was 24 hours before she could finally break the news to him, and both had to endure another week of doubt and conjecture before Blyth's eyeball-to-eyeball confrontation with Phillips on Hobart's Constitution Dock eventually revealed the hoax.

Cat's cradle: ropes hold up Hofbräu Lager's mast as she arrives in Hobart, the crew spent the last days anxiously listening to ominous creaks and groans

Nuclear Electric finally reached the Derwent River on 4 January, some 20 hours ahead of Commercial Union and two weeks ahead of the race schedule. It was as much a triumph for conservatism as a victory over the fleet, and Chittenden said of his safety-first approach: "I did predict damage to the other boats if they pushed too hard and that happened. It has been quite hard on us too and many of my crew are really tired."

Speaking after his first hot bath for 49 days, but before closer inspection of his yacht had found a kink in the mast and a crack running down the entire length of her keel, the skipper reflected: "These boats are absolutely brilliant going to windward in strong winds. I was a bit apprehensive when the first depression hit us after Cape Horn. I had not sailed the yacht to windward in such strong winds before and it cost us six hours learning how to sail her at her best."

He also revealed that while other crews tensioned their rigging in Rio in readiness for the battle to windward that lay ahead, the Nuclear Electric skipper had slackened his shrouds. "My father always told me to take two turns off the bottle-screws during the winter months to take account of the cold weather," Chittenden explained.

What did surprise him was the competitiveness shown by his amateur crew. "They have all been very successful in business and joined this race for a new challenge in life. They are all very competitive, gave 110 per cent effort and it was difficult sometimes to hold them back. They always wanted to wind the boat up and I had to stop them, otherwise we would have

First among equals.

Energy for the 21st Century

After 151 days and 28,000 miles of one of the most ruelling sea-going challenges known to Man, our boat came in.

We are delighted to salute skipper John Chittenden and is gallant crew on winning the British Steel Challenge round e world race.

It was a performance characterised by highly professional leadership and steady, safety-first progress coupled with teamwork and a steely determination to win.

We salute also the other nine crews and their fine individual achievements.

In such an enthralling contest, we were proud and delighted to play a leading part.

Nuclear Electric

CLEAN ENERGY FOR THE 21ST CENTURY

smashed our rig up too."

The most frightening aspect of the voyage had not been the high seas and hurricane force winds, but the ice. "We could not pick up the growlers on radar, and at night we went frighteningly close to some chunks. We missed two of them by less than a boat length, one standing 20ft high, the other the size of Westminster Abbey," he told us.

Richard Merriweather was equal in praise for his crew. "I've inherited a great team. They were just dying to change things when I joined them in Rio and they were prepared to work hard. We are obviously disappointed not to have won because we thought for a long time that we could, but we were beaten fair and square. It was a great race and we could not have pushed any harder."

Rhône-Poulenc supplied all the yachts with a comprehensive medical kit

For CU crewman Eric Gustavson, a plastic surgeon, the harshness of the Southern Ocean was the most testing part of the voyage. "The cold and the damp have been so extreme that had the QE2 turned up with berths at £10,000 each, all 14 of us might have been tempted to jump ship," he said.

Twenty-five hours later, as British Steel II reached Wellington to refuel for the final 1,000 mile stage across the Tasman, Hofbräu Lager limped into port with a cat's-cradle of ropes and wire supporting her badly damaged mast. Goss and his crew had found a crack extending 85 per cent around the mast section just above deck level three days before. Goss said: "The biggest problem was when the boat started to pitch in the seas and the mast began to rotate." Crewman Steve Rigby admitted: "It was pretty scary. We were really lucky. The crack was opening and closing more than 5mm at times and the mast creaked and groaned every time the boat fell off a wave. No one has slept for the past 48 hours!"

Coopers & Lybrand stormed up the Derwent under spinnaker seven hours later, her crew oblivious to the fact that their mast was in an even worse state than Hofbräu's. Cherry's crew were followed by Group 4 which finally pipped Ian MacGillivray's Pride of Teesside by three hours after trading places, often within sight of each other during the previous week.

Paul Jeffes and his InterSpray crew were a disappointed eighth, finishing 500 miles ahead of Rhône-Poulenc, but they consoled themselves by retaining second place overall until the independent jury awarded generous time allowances to those crews who had diverted to assist British Steel II.

The same jury also made a controversial ruling not to penalise Tudor and his crew for motoring the 3,000 miles to Hobart, a decision that was to reverberate around Constitution Dock throughout the fleet's stay in Hobart.

LEG 2 DAMAGE REPORT

BRITISH STEEL II

Watch leader Yvonne Flatman and David Arthur confined to their bunks for first ten days after contracting food poisoning in Rio.

16 December. Dismasted in mid-ocean 2,000 miles from nearest land. Heath Insured and Group 4 crews divert to hand fuel across. Crew erect jury rig and motor sail to

Hobart via Chatham Island and Wellington, after picking up a further 1,000 litres of fuel from container ship New Zealand Pacific.

RHÔNE-POULENC

Cap shroud tangs bent during violent broach resulting in slackened rigging. Yacht diverted to Port Stanley, Falkland Islands to collect new bolt, rigging and spreaders flown out by the RAF. Two crew badly bruised about their faces by flailing ropes when yacht was tacked by a large wave.

COOPERS & LYBRAND

Phil Jones, British Steel one-legger from Port Talbot, experienced continuous seasickness. Geraint Lewis suffered broken collarbone when thrown out of bunk by a wave. Yacht suffered broken forestay bottle-screw. On inspection at Hobart, yacht found to have large crack in mast at deck level.

GROUP 4 SECURITAS

First to experience broken forestay bottle-screw and diverted to Florianopolis, Brazil to pick up replacement flown out by courier from England. New bottle-screw failed 2,000 miles later.

HOFBRÄU LAGER

Broken bottle-screw led to crack extending 85 per cent around mast at deck level. Watch leader Jack Gordon Smith suffered cracked ribs after being thrown across yacht. Hit whale but escaped damage.

HEATH INSURED

Broken bottle-screw and steering cables.

INTERSPRAY.

Broken bottle-screw. Watch leader John Davis injured when spinnaker pole crashed down on his head.

COMMERCIAL UNION

Eric Gustavson broke rib. Sue Tight suffered bad rope burns to her hands. Yacht suffered torn sail, damaged pulpit and bent wheel.

NUCLEAR ELECTRIC

Broken staysail sheet. In Hobart, mast found to be badly bent and keel cracked.

CHAPTER FIVE

"Storm After Storm"

Riding the
Roaring Forties

Inevitably, Blyth and his team received

stinging criticism for the forestay problems experienced on six of the yachts during the previous stage round Cape Horn. The strongest came in the form of an editorial in the Guardian newspaper:

"The risks associated with the British Steel Challenge were well known: this was the race in which the amateurs could screw up so badly that lives might be lost. But once the fog which still hangs over the shambolic second leg from Rio to Hobart clears, it is not the amateurs who will be called into account; it will be the professionals who must explain how and why they failed the amateurs so badly."

"We've been washed, spun but certainly not dried", was how one crewman put it. Here Commercial Union dries out in Hobart at the end of the second leg from Rio

Norseman-Gibb, which manufactured the broken bottle-screws, side-stepped the issue by stating that they had merely provided what had been specified on the drawings. Designer David Thomas was equally quick to clear his yardarm: "I was not involved in designing the rig or invited on any of the trials," he said, revealing the rift that had developed between him and Blyth's building team during early stages of construction.

Matthew Sheehan, technical editor of Yachting World, and former rigger, wrote an informed article in the February issue of the British magazine highlighting the fact that the 14mm Dyform wire, made up of specially shaped strands to allow closer packing, had a higher breaking strain (19,300kg) than the 7/8in clevis pins rated at only 14,200kg, which connected the bottle-screws to the deck fitting. An additional factor, he suggested, was that the steel hulls have less "give" in them than a glassfibre or wooden hull, which would result in a greater proportion of shock loadings being transmitted to the rig.

Andrew Roberts, the hapless project director, agreed he had been responsible for specifying the bottle-screws but, in his defence, Blyth pointed out that five other specialists, including the designer, rigger, mast and bottle-screw manufacturer, had all seen the drawings, and not questioned any of the specifications.

The arguments were complicated further by the fact that Nuclear Electric, with the slackest rigging within the fleet, and Commercial Union with the tightest settings, had not suffered any failures.

Andrew Cawley, the technical manager at Norseman-Gibb, flew down to Hobart to examine the broken parts. His report, published on 5 February, ten days before the fleet set off into the Southern Ocean again, pointed to several other factors not highlighted in the press.

The first was the use of a two-foot-long bar used as a lever by the Group 4 crew in Rio, instead of a spanner, to put extra tension in the rig. The report stated: "Failure analysis confirmed that the rigging screw had fractured in fatigue due to the high initial tension applied, aggravated by the additional in-service load variations. Approximately 30 per cent of the fracture surface area was fatigued and the balance was caused by ductile tensile failure."

After inspecting the other broken-screws, Cawley concluded that all six had failed in a similar manner, half through fatigue, and the balance through ductile tensile failure. The cause, he suggested, was not the size of the bottle-screw, but the fact that the fastening positions between the forestay and headsail tack were so close that the shackle holding down the sail had prevented the screw from articulating correctly, thus increasing fatigue levels to the point of failure. He also noted that the practice of binding the screws and toggles with amalgam tape to prevent chafing had exacerbated the problem.

By then heavier wire and larger bottle-screws had already been shipped out from England and fitted to the ten yachts as a belt-and-braces solution to the problems. Blyth concluded: "That decision had to be made in mid-December and based on information available at that time. It would not necessarily be the same now."

Another mystery the technicians within the fleet had to solve was the vertical crack discovered running down the centre of Nuclear Electric's 12-tonne cast iron keel when the yacht was pulled out of the water for inspection. Samples sent to a laboratory to identify the cause suggested that the failure was not one related to stresses generated within the hull during the race, but a casting failure.

Divers, who went down to inspect the nine other yachts within the fleet, gave their keels a clean bill of health, while John Cox recalled a day in Rio just prior to the restart when they were sitting in the cockpit and were startled by a sudden unexplained bang within the boat. "We think the keel must have cracked on its own accord then," he suggested.

Roberts was quick to allay further fears for the fleet."The keel may be cracked, but it is in no danger of falling off. I always knew these boats were immensely strong but to see one showing keel damage being sailed into first place, shows just how strong and safe they are." He then arranged for the keel to be repaired under the supervision of a Bureau Veritas surveyor by welding half inch plates across either side of the damage.

If the bottle-screw saga had not been enough, Blyth and his men faced more brickbats, this time over an unexplained decision taken by the International Yacht Racing Union jury not to penalise the British Steel II crew for motoring the 3,000 miles across the Pacific to Hobart. In doing so the independent committee turned the cardinal rule against motoring during a race on its head, leaving the yachting establishment in both hemispheres dumbfounded, and rival crews deeply aggrieved.

Shell-shocked perhaps by the attacks over the bottle-screws, Blyth ducked for cover. His press team issued only the result of the hearing and not the findings of the jury, and the

> *"The keel may be cracked, but it is in no danger of falling off."*

man himself refused to discuss the matter. As a result, the cynics back home were given further ammunition to ridicule the event as a staged adventure, not a race.

Yet the men who decided the issue were all leading international judges with experience of ruling over major events like the America's Cup and Sydney-Hobart race. The rules they had to preside over were those of the IYRU with supplements copied wholesale from the 20-year-old Whitbread Round the World race. It was one of their rules, allowing a disabled yacht to motor to the nearest port, make repairs, and then rejoin the race, that was central to the argument.

The jury ruled that this applied equally if the port of call was further down the leg, or even the finish. In doing so, however, they ignored the precedents set during past Whitbread races when disabled yachts had been given some measure of penalty, unless they returned to the point of disaster before resuming to race.

Ian Bailey Wilmot, the Whitbread race director, was among those who disagreed with the outcome. "The British Steel crew was afforded a lot of outside assistance, not least from the P&O ship which dropped off 1,000 litres of fuel. They were given further help in Chatham Island and Wellington. I can see no circumstances in which the yacht would have escaped a penalty in the Whitbread race."

The jury also appeared to ignore the fact that three of the British Steel II crew left the yacht at Chatham Island and Wellington to take holidays. That in itself is not against the rules though it must be hard now for Giles Trollope and his two friends, Patrick Quinn and Rob Haine, to reconcile themselves to the fact that they did not complete their circumnavigation. What was seen to be against the rules was that Richard Tudor took on two replacements in Keith Mundell and Vicky Gladwell during the refuelling stop at Wellington for the final stage of the voyage across the Tasman to Hobart.

Tudor turned off his engine 100 metres from the line and sailed across to claim an elapsed time from Rio. He was adamant that he and his crew had done everything according to the book and should not be penalised for motoring 3,500 miles. The jury agreed

Speech bubble: SOMETHING TELLS ME THEY LIKED US

CAPE TOWN

Tudor gained permission for them to be on board from a race official, but this, other crews were convinced, was given the nod only because everyone believed they had retired.

It came as some surprise therefore when Richard Tudor calmly turned off British Steel's engine 100 metres from the finish and sailed unaided across the line - as the rules require - to claim a finish time.

In coming to their controversial decision, the jury ignored the committee's suggestion that the yacht should be penalised two days and barred from competing for the overall prize. (Blyth, so we learned after the fleet had left Hobart, had pressed for a five-day penalty). Instead, the jury decided that since British Steel had averaged only 4.1 knots - against 7 knots set by their sailing rivals - they had gained no advantage from motoring, and therefore should not have a penalty.

Peter Phillips, who was not alone in his opposition, said: "I don't agree with this decision and think it has made a joke out of the race." His only hope was that the issue would be quickly forgotten once the fleet got under way again.

The chorus of dissenting voices within the fleet was so strong that Blyth was forced to distribute a four-page letter of explanation to the crews. It did not address the issue of the changing crew list and did nothing to quell the furore. There was not even agreement within Tudor's own crew with David

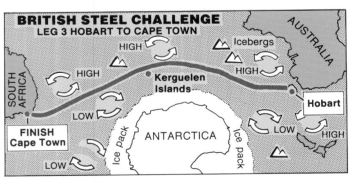

BRITISH STEEL CHALLENGE
LEG 3 HOBART TO CAPE TOWN

AUSTRALIA

HIGH

Icebergs

HIGH

SOUTH AFRICA

HIGH

Kerguelen Islands

HIGH

Hobart

LOW

ANTARCTICA

Ice pack

Ice pack

LOW

HIGH

FINISH Cape Town

LOW

Arthur openly expressing his view that the yacht should have retired.

Some crews became so steamed up over the issue that two teams became just as open in talking of taking advantage of any small breakages experienced during the next leg to

motor through calms to ensure that they were first into Cape Town. But with no power of appeal, neither competitors' nor Blyth's race committee could raise the issue again.

Where people-power did claim a significant victory, however, was over a change of course proposed by Blyth to keep the yachts out of the worst of the Roaring Forties. Concerned by the damage sustained to the fleet during the last stage round Cape Horn, the organisers decided to ask the crews about re-routeing the fleet around Amsterdam Island, 450 miles north of the planned course, well away from the icebergs and strong winds then plaguing the solo Globe Challenge yachts racing round the world in the opposite direction.

"When we took up this Challenge, most of us knew what to expect," said Adrian Rayson, one of the 105 people to have paid the full £15,000 to race right round the world. "We don't want people now watering this down or moving the goal posts just because of a few difficulties experienced by some yachts during the last stage."

It was a view shared by an overwhelming 82 per cent of the people taking part who voted to stick to the tough course

Sail damage: Vince Hughes with some of Commercial Union's sails. Crews were penalised for sails lost or destroyed

originally charted across the Southern Ocean to Cape Town via the isolated French outpost of Kerguelen Island.

A planned change of mainsails at this midway stage of the race was also discarded. "The original sails remain in remarkably good condition and the skippers have agreed to retain them," Roberts announced a week before the restart. Even British Steel II sailed with the mainsail her crew had managed to salvage, patched up with a new head rather than renewed. "A new sail would have been the cheaper option, but would have given the crew an unfair advantage," Roberts added.

This too was welcomed by a majority within the fleet who had begun this race believing that they had to make their sails last the entire 28,000 miles. "The original ethos of this race, placing strong emphasis on sail care, prudence and seamanship would have been lost if sails that have been blown out are now replaced," Rayson argued.

But while the new mainsails were kept in their bags and shipped to Cape Town as possible replacements for the last stage back to Southampton, the ten crews were issued with new staysails. "These sails have taken quite a battering and this change had been planned from the outset," said Roberts.

To reinforce this stand on sail care, both British Steel II and InterSpray were forced to sail an extra distance eastward when the fleet left Hobart on 13 February as a penalty for destroying sails during the previous stage. Richard Tudor and his crew had an extra 17 miles to cover, but InterSpray, which led the fleet out of the Derwent River, had to cover almost double that distance after losing a bigger sail.

> "I think we got off lightly on the last leg round Cape Horn"

It proved a mighty handicap distance. When Jeffes and his crew finally turned south, the leaders had already broken away, riding under spinnaker on the back of a north-westerly frontal system.

While the rigging difficulties and protests may have made headlines back home, life in Hobart was far from acrimonious. Indeed, for many this Tasmanian stopover became the favourite port of call, a point captured in a cartoon published in the Hobart Mercury.

One who has an enduring memory of the place is Rod Street, the 49-year-old property renovator from Gloucester, sailing on board Rhône-Poulenc. His continual bragging at evading the Poll Tax and reminders that had awaited his arrival both at Rio and Hobart, prompted Peter Phillips to organise another of his famous pranks, this time involving the local police chief. Street was taken totally by surprise when the police arrived on the dock one morning with orders to arrest him for non-payment of the tax. He was led away hand-cuffed, and convinced that he was about to be deported. Instead of being driven to the police station, however, the forlorn-looking yachtsman was driven to the hospitality tent at the Hobart Gold Cup race meeting, where the police chief welcomed him, still hand-cuffed, with a glass of champagne.

The Rhône-Poulenc crewman did have the last laugh, however, for while he was tucking into the smoked salmon and bubbly, Phillips and his crew had to buy their own drinks in the public bar.

When reviewing this 6,300-mile stage across the Indian Ocean, John Chittenden pulled no punches with his crew. "I think we got off lightly on the last leg round Cape Horn. I expect this leg to be a lot tougher," he warned.

Indeed, the forecasts offered the strong prospect of westerly gales pounding the fleet for much of course. Adding to their problems, Alan Wynne Thomas, the Welsh solo yachtsman who had retired to Hobart from the Globe Challenge race after sustaining six broken ribs in a fall, warned of numerous icebergs as high as 40 degrees South.

Despite these pessimistic predictions, there were only three unscheduled changes among the 130 recruits. John Kirk, a 49-year-old outdoor activities instructor on Coopers & Lybrand, was sidelined by an old back injury and replaced by Martin Wright from Helensburgh. Michael Calvin, the Daily Telegraph's man-at-the-scene, returned for a second bite of the cherry after Hofbräu's Michael Kay, the salesman within the race organisation, was ordered back to base to drum up sponsorship for the next race planned for 1996/97.

The final change was the inclusion of Bill St Leger, a fire fighter and paramedic with the local Hobart brigade, who abandoned a bush fire raging just outside the town to take up the spare medic's berth on Nuclear Electric.

Reviewing the course, where icebergs, headwinds and intense cold would be the principal enemies, Ken Pearson, a watch leader aboard Heath Insured, predicted to his crew: "This time it is straight out into the Southern Ocean. It will be a big shock after the hospitality of Hobart, and the boat that is best prepared for this will take the lead."

One attractive alternative thrown up by the weather patterns was to ride the reaching winds of a high pressure system then centred over the Australian Bight. "It's tempting" admitted Chittenden. "The diversion would add 400 miles to the course, meaning we would have to gain an extra 60 miles each day during the first week, but we would be sailing in warmer and much more pleasant conditions." In the end, herding instincts prevailed. The yachts rode south in a close pack, each crew determined to keep tabs on their closest rivals.

The departure from Hobart was special. Thousands came down to the dockside to say farewell and most then crowded onto everything from ferries to beach catamarans to chase the fleet down the Derwent River. Indeed, so many spectator craft straddled the start line when the gun fired that it was the race yachts that had to weave in and out to avoid collisions.

Richard Merriweather had Commercial Union's bows across the line first followed by Nuclear Electric and Group 4. By the first bend in the river it was apparent that Paul Jeffes' crew on Interspray had successfully avoided the crush and gained considerably from their solitary course away from the spectator fleet.

Within 24 hours Commercial Union and Nuclear Electric were back in their now customary position at the head of the fleet, having opened up an 80-mile advantage over the tail-enders on InterSpray. By contrast, Group 4 was sixth, just 18 miles behind the leaders.

After some six weeks in port, all the yachts suffered from rusty routines. Reporting from Commercial Union, Sue Tight admitted: "Johnny Norton got caught up the mast this morning while trying to thread the reefing pennants. The halyard seized and he spent the next half hour swinging around with the motion of the boat while we motivated ourselves to get him down."

On board Coopers & Lybrand, Vivien Cherry's sewing circle was hastily reformed to repair the damaged spinnaker, ripped all the way round one leech and most of the way across the foot. "Everybody is either stitching or sticking. At a repair rate of two feet an hour, we have another two to three days to go," she reported.

By 16 February, Heath Insured had elbowed her way into the lead after experiencing stronger winds to the north of the

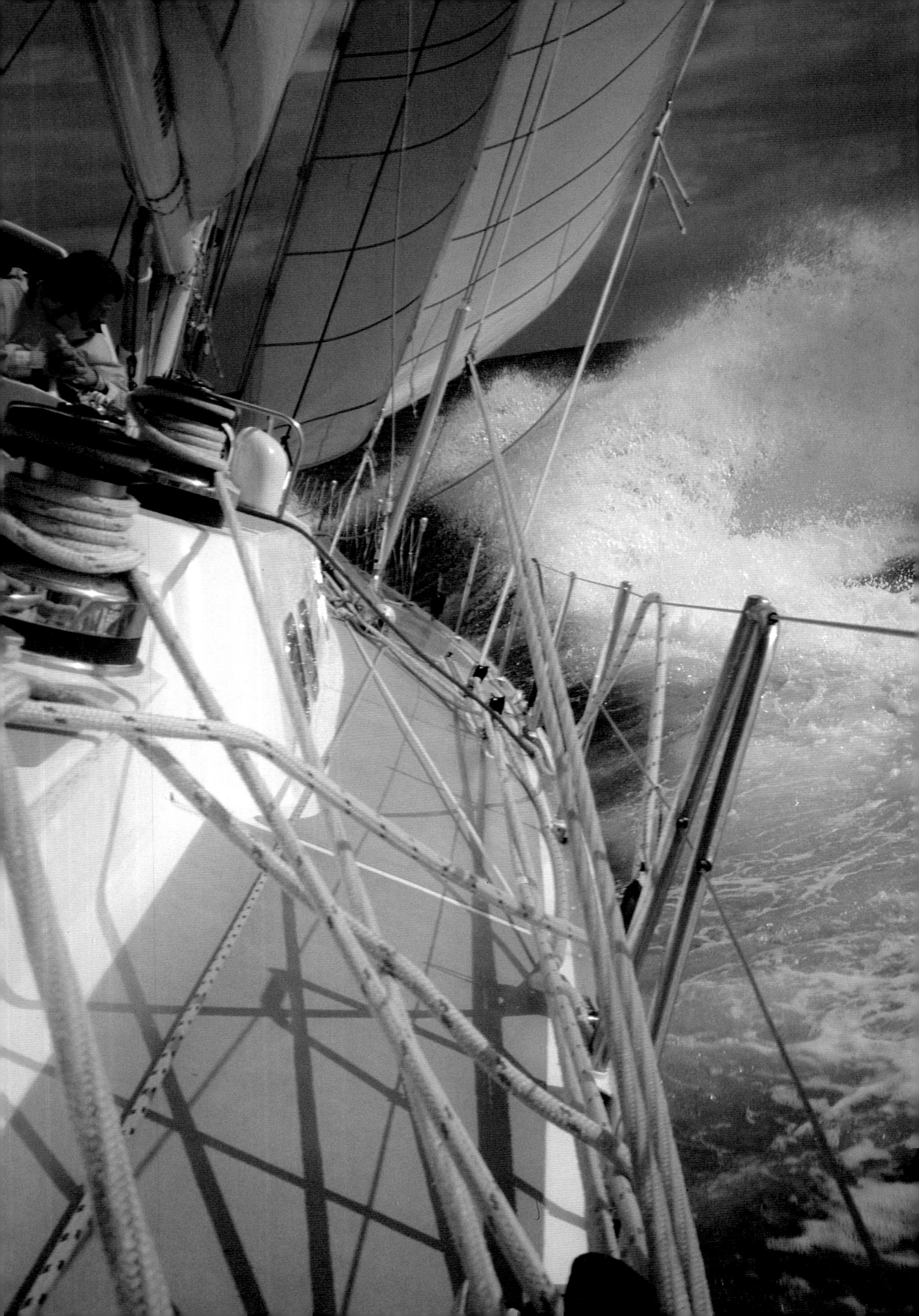

British Steel II finds the going tough. Foredeck work was highly dangerous and caused many injuries

fleet which was now spread out over a 120-mile front. Pride of Teesside, one of the most southerly yachts, now dragging her stern in ninth place, was duty yacht. Reporting on the news that day, skipper Ian MacGillivray showed that he, at least, had not lost his sense of humour. With certain glee, he passed on the news that Roger Peek, the treasurer at British Steel plc, sailing this leg on InterSpray "Had his first taste of the Southern Ocean today - most of it inside his wet weather gear!"

By 18 February, five days into the race, the positions changed once more with the wind, dumping Heath back to fourth and handing the lead back to Chittenden and his crew. Adrian "Radio" Rayson, busily soaking up the atmosphere, remained unfazed by this set-back. "Nature has put on a glorious display tonight," he reported to the world. "The sky is alive with the Southern lights with vast curtains of pastel-coloured hues adorning the heavens. Elsewhere, strong beams of blue pierce the sky. A trip to the Planetarium in London will never be the same again!"

"Down below, the galley is festooned with fresh vegetables and nets of fruit. 'I'm just popping out for a couple of onions,' Carol Randall told us as she prepared lunch yesterday. 'Sounds like she is off down the garden' quipped Arthur Haynes as she headed off to a far corner of the boat. It doesn't stop at fruit and veg. Cheese, meat pies and more cakes than you can shake a stick at, swell the larders. Life on board is good. But on deck more clothing is being donned as temperatures drop and increasing amounts of sea thrash down over the bows."

It was one of these waves that led to the first injury of this leg. Pete Goss flashed an urgent message back to Race HQ from eighth-placed Hofbräu Lager stating: "Steve Rigby has fallen against the wheel and injured his left arm. The elbow is swollen and Jonathan Myers, our on-board doctor, has put it in a sling. It may be a hairline fracture but it is probably badly bruised."

That same day, Mike Golding and his men on Group 4 Securitas began their run to the front after taking a middle route within the fleet. Their advantage, initially, was a mere nine miles over Nuclear Electric as the first wave of depressions hit. During the following week Group 4 slowly began to pull away. But it remained a close fight, and Golding knew full well that the slightest mistake would drag them back in among the pursuing pack again.

By 20 February, six days into the leg, 20 miles was all that separated the four front runners; Group 4, Rhône-Poulenc,

Commercial Union and Chittenden's Nuclear Electric. Richard Merriweather gave the first inkling of how far conditions had deteriorated. "Making good progress, but the seas are huge and the foredeck is awash," he reported.

Peter Phillips, now up at the front for the first time, was making most of the cut and thrust. "It's nail-biting. Every 12-hourly chat show reveals positions changing constantly by very small margins. Being three miles ahead of another yacht is considered a luxury at this end of the fleet. This must be the closest racing ever in long distance events. It is as though we were dinghy racing!"

Chittenden's yacht had dropped to fourth, but there were no signs of concern within the master mariner's message: "Strong winds have continued for four days. Now cold and southerly. The heaters are on and we are now down to staysail and second reef in the main. The new forestay gives great confidence and there are no worries about the keel," he told race officials.

A day later and the green water sweeping over Group 4 Securitas was so great that it set off a worldwide alert when water activated one of the crew's man-overboard distress beacons. The signal was picked up first by the Australian rescue authorities at Canberra, but Golding quickly calmed their fears by notifying both Race HQ and the coastguard at Falmouth of the false alarm. These water-triggered alarms, carried by each crew in the pockets of their oilskins, were prototypes for a new safety system designed to pinpoint a crewman swept overboard.

These false alarms were a continual problem throughout this Southern Ocean stage as water, running waist deep across the deck, swept the crew off their feet. It is one that has still to be resolved by the manufacturers, but to everyone fighting to keep a tenuous hold down in the depths of the Screaming Fifties, these false alarms did at least reassure everyone that if they did

Storm after storm: "On deck it is cold and wet.. Below verticals and horizontals fight with each other," was how one crewman described the Southern Ocean

fall overboard, the damned things worked!

Another safety problem, this time the failure of Rhône-Poulenc's masthead navigation lights during the first week at sea, led to full-time lookouts posted on deck until Jerry Walsingham braved the sickening gyrations of the masthead to fix them. "It was a difficult job in a nasty sea and by the time he came down, Jerry felt like he had done a couple of rounds with Frank Bruno!," Phillips reported.

By now, the proximity of the magnetic pole was causing a

certain amount of confusion on board the yachts. Compasses had become so sluggish that they gave little inkling of the course to be steered. "It's proving a particular problem at night," complained Pete Goss.

On 24 February, 11 days into this leg, Golding's men had opened up a 20-mile advantage over their leading rivals as the fleet reached the halfway stage between Hobart and the Kerguelen Islands. With the exception of Group 4, the rest of the fleet was racing almost line abreast across a 180-mile band between 51 and 54 degrees South.

On board Heath Insured, the most northerly yacht now back in seventh place, Rayson reported: "Thirty knots of wind and confused seas. We have been crashing along for several days and on deck it is cold and wet. Below, verticals and horizontals fight with each other. Things fly out of cupboards and drinks leap out of mugs. Crew now eat standing up and wet kit hangs autumnally round."

"The foredeck crew, working to change headsails, are lashed by breaking seas. Expletives rend the air, but the eyes have it - bright, flashing and determined. The night is now falling. The wind is gusting to 40 knots and the boat is bucking like a wild horse. God knows why, but hails of laughter bounce around the deck. It should not make sense but it does. This is life led by a new set of rules. These are the sounds of a crew working at a higher plane."

Peter Phillips was also fighting a losing battle to keep his balance. "My greatest fear has been of someone being thrown around and injured down below. It happened on other yachts during the last leg, and an hour ago while moving through the cabin, I lost my footing and struck my head. I was wearing specs; the frames broke and a piece jabbed into my face near my right eye. There was a lot of blood but no damage - I'm hard headed."

Worse was to come the following day as Paul Jeffes, whose InterSpray had by now recovered to sixth place, reported: "We are experiencing the roughest conditions of the voyage so far. Winds up to 70 knots; extremely large waves frequently breaking right over the boat, making deck work very hazardous indeed. Last night, during a routine operation to replace a broken storm staysail sheet, we had three minor injuries on deck. I've now instructed Julian Wells, the ship's doctor - not noted for excessive sympathy to the sick and suffering - to issue no more sick notes. Just death certificates...."

"Forecasters say we can expect another two days of this, and whilst I would like to go north, the other tack is simply not a proposition in this wind direction. This route, complete with icebergs, gales and monster waves of water below -3 degrees Centigrade is, regrettably, the right way to go. It is not a popular decision, especially with the on-watch now sitting up top in a blizzard!"

On board Rhône-Poulenc, Phillips' crew was enduring a similar battle for survival. The skipper's log reads:

Wednesday 24 February
0500 Blowing very hard with vicious seas and freezing spray across the deck, lashing everyone.
Down below it is evil. Can hardly stand and everything is wet. People are running out of dry clothes.
Wind still rising and suddenly hits 49 knots - sails are quickly dropped in appalling conditions. Paul Egan and Nick Fenner were washed along the deck and thrown several feet in the air by the seas. Paul

TEES✝SIDE

AROUND THE WORLD WITH PRIDE

From Southampton to Rio de Janeiro, from Rio to Hobart, from Hobart to Cape Town, from Cape Town to Southampton... fighting the seas, battling the storms... more than 30,000 miles completed of the British Steel Challenge Round the World Yacht Race.

Ten identical boats competing in the toughest yacht race ever.

One boat, however, is different from the rest. Pride of Teesside is carrying the hopes and aspirations of an entire region of the United Kingdom.

Sponsored by the Teesside Development Corporation, the largest of the UK government's urban regeneration agencies, the yacht is a symbol of the confident resurgence of this corner of the North East of England.

The scale and pace of change on Teesside is enormous with imaginative development projects

creating new homes, modern industries, improved leisure and educational facilities... some of the largest urban regeneration schemes in Europe taking place right now... attracting inward investment from commercial and industrial concerns around the world.

Teesdale, a £500 million mixed use development three times the size of London's Canary Wharf... a £160 million marina at Hartlepool... a brand new university college... a £50 million barrage across the River Tees...

The changing face of Teesside.

A region with a proud history... a region with a 21st Century future.

DEVELOPMENT CORPORATION

For futher details contact: Duncan Hall Chief Executive, Teesside Development Corporation, Dunedin House, Riverside Quay, Stockton-on-Tees, Cleveland, United Kingdom, TS17 6BJ. Tel: (0642) 677123. Fax: (0642) 676123.

Autohelm ST 50.
It lets you start small.

And think big.

openly admitted he had been scared.

1500 We were hit by a long sustained gust of 62 knots. Simon Walker managed to turn the yacht downwind and save the sails and we went back over our course at 11.4 knots. Ridiculous, but exactly the right action to take. We got the third reef in the main and the storm jib on. Great work by everyone.

1900 Bad news. RP back to sixth place. British Steel II and Hofbräu Lager have passed us and all the others have closed up.

Wind over 50 knots, gusting to 75-80 knots at times over some of the fleet. Nuclear Electric has shredded her staysail and Hofbräu has lost her steering - All good fun really!

Thursday 25 February
Simon Walker's 25th birthday.

Last night could have been tragedy but for people doing the right things and thinking about safety all the time.

Nick Atha had just clipped his safety harness on the jackstay when a huge wave struck the boat. It picked Nick up and threw him across the cockpit to the leeward side, over the cockpit coaming and headfirst out through the guard rails. His head and shoulders were out through the rails when his harness line went tight.

The wave had laid the yacht over and Nick's head was under water. As the yacht came back up, he was hauled to the safety of the cockpit. His legs were like jelly and he knew it had been a close thing.

Shortly after, the yacht was thrown on its side again and all the forward stanchions were bent to 45 degrees.

0700 Chat Show. Thank Christ for good news. We have taken some miles out of every boat in the fleet. Pulled back a little on Group 4, a lot on Commercial Union, and Nuclear electric and Hofbräu are within

nine miles ahead. The rest have been pushed back, so now we are happy people again. When racing this close, everyone gets edgy waiting for the next chat-show positions, but it is great stuff!

The next 24 hours were the worst of the whole race with 70-knot+ headwinds and huge seas lashing the entire fleet. On board the fifth-placed British Steel II riding 78 miles behind Group 4, Kevin Dufficy wrote home: "Seventy-mile-an-hour winds are laced with ice. If your skin is exposed you get lacerated. Waves bigger than houses approach and you think it's curtains, but the boat forges into the wave and 10ft of water buries the yacht and crew from stem to stern. Gasping for breath, you think we won't come up, but slowly, so slowly, the water clears enough to see the next house wave coming. We have three crew members on deck for 15 minutes each. Any more and the cold is likely to cause hypothermia. Do your job like clockwork, don't think about the battering of the waves or the pain of the cold. Too cold even to take off the dry-suit. You just climb into your bunk, boots and all, to catch a few moments sleep before the next call."

"Scared? No, but terrified every time you go up. The achievement is to overcome that fear and the greatest motivation is not to let down your crew mates. Optimistically, we look for a respite in the weather, but Giles Trollope has looked at the weather fax and says, 'You ain't seen nothing yet!'"

On Pride of Teesside, now 153 miles behind the leaders Ian MacGillivray's crew were, according to their skipper, "revelling

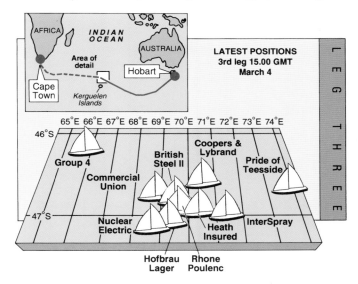

in the experience if a little apprehensive". He continued: "The waves have started to take on the proportions of the rolling English Downs with the odd Matterhorn thrown in to make life interesting. The surfaces of the waves are covered with white foaming streaks along with larger white patches where the crests have tumbled off. These crests are around the size of a haystack and when one breaks over the boat, everything except the mast seems to disappear in a white foaming mass of freezing water."

"A night watch in these conditions means straining one's ears and eyes into the blackness, trying to work out where the next wave will come aboard to soak you through to the skin. The water finds its way through every small gap in the protective clothing and you sustain yourself knowing that below, the warm womb of the boat awaits."

During this period, Coopers & Lybrand pulled up two places to seventh after setting an amazing average of 10.4 knots during one six-hour period - though at some cost to her crew. In one of her regular dispatches to The Times, skipper Vivien Cherry wrote: "Our cockpit acrobatics team now includes Matt Steel-Jessop, Samantha Wood, David Turner, Bertie Griffith, Arnie Malmberg and myself who are all sporting a variety of bruises and swellings. Our show-stopping stunt is the inverted wheel-spin - a very stylish manoeuvre, but one in which the landings still require practice."

"We have taken to naming the wave types. Along with the 'Bellyflop' and 'Mountain', is the 'Galley Growler', the 'Bunk Bouncer', and after the 'Smoker Soaker' comes the 'Stern Whip' and 'Corkscrew'. The 'Stern Whip' breaks over the stern quarter to give whoever is at the wheel a real soaking. The ultimate, however, is the 'Corkscrew', since there is no warning - and no way out!"

Mike Golding and his Group 4 men reached the Kerguelen Islands on 3 March, having built up a 94-mile advantage over Nuclear Electric and Hofbräu Lager which were within five miles of each other fighting for second place. Despite the conditions - the harshest in the race - Golding's men had set an average of more than seven knots over the first 3,700-mile stage of the voyage, and if they maintained this pace to the Cape of Good Hope, could have finished by 16 March, ten days ahead of schedule.

But the weather had more to throw at the fleet. Rhône-Poulenc's log read:

Friday 5 March
0900 Weather is absolute shit. Blowing 40 knots with driving rain and sleet. Still trucking along at 8 knots.
1900 Chat Show. Very good news. Pulled miles back on all those in front, 18 from Group 4; 9 off Nuclear Electric, 6 off Commercial Union and 1 from Hofbrau which is now only 4 miles in front and a special target.
Had a great battle with British Steel II in the night. At one stage she was only 0.6 mile behind us and we could see her just off our starboard quarter. In only half an hour, we pulled 2.3 miles in front which was visual on our radar. All great stuff and unheard of in ocean racing after sailing thousands of miles.

Three days later Ian MacGillivray, whose yacht had been within three miles of the British Antarctic survey vessel HMS Discovery when her crew reported a 27-metre wave, told a local radio station on Teesside: "We have cracks on either side of the skeg which have been leaking. We've cured the leak for the moment, but we haven't cured the cracks. We are just hoping we don't get a really big storm again and the skeg perhaps breaks off and sinks the boat. The only thing we can do is press on and hopefully get to Cape Town, then get the boat lifted out of the water before it gets too bad."

The two-inch crack on one side of the skeg was a recurrence of an earlier problem uncovered at Hobart. There, the damage had been deemed "superficial" by the Bureau Veritas surveyor. "There was nothing to suggest now that the problem is any more serious," said Andrew Roberts, the Race director. "We are obviously concerned and have asked the crew to check the extent of the cracks each day, but the skeg and rudder assembly is massively over-engineered. It is highly unlikely that the skeg would fall off because the rudder stock is strong enough to support it," he assured.

But, as a precaution, the Teesside crew headed northwards into warmer waters to avoid the worst of the weather battering the rest of the fleet. In doing so they lost around 250 miles on the leaders. It was a diversion that coincided with a fishy story of Teesside's crew catching a 40kg tuna on a line towed behind the yacht. Indeed, it was so large, we were told, that the crew had to stop their yacht for 15 minutes just to land it, and were forced by the smell to throw the carcass back overboard three days later, having been unable to consume it all.

The story generated several laughs within the fleet, not least when this crew was awarded the safety prize for their act of self preservation. As Ian MacGillivray went up to collect his trophy at the prize giving in Cape Town, a rival crewman was heard to quip: "Safety be dammed. They only turned north because the tuna were running that way!"

This move north did have an unexpected payback, however, for the day after turning away from the southern swells, Pride of Teesside reduced the deficit on ninth-placed InterSpray by 18 miles.

Over 630 miles further south, Hofbräu Lager was battling to retain third place from Rhône-Poulenc, then just three miles further from Cape Town. Skipper Pete Goss reported: "This is perhaps the worst storm yet. The seas are particularly bad and we are constantly laid over with all winches under water. One wave had all the books across the saloon and into the supper!"

At the same time, the crew on Heath Insured were repairing the steering for the third time during this race. One-legger Jonathan Goodall reflected: "Having experienced the problems before, the crew knew exactly what to do. We are now making eight knots into a heavy swell, the 40-ton steel hull reverberating as she thuds into a wave or tumbles 30ft off another. Ironically, just 24 hours earlier, we were drifting backwards at 1.5 knots, totally becalmed. This race has a bit of everything."

By 17 March, Group 4's lead appeared secure as Golding and his men closed to within 350 miles of Cape Town, leaving

> *"We have cracks on either side of the skeg which have been leaking. We've cured the leak for the moment, but we haven't cured the cracks."*

Cape Town crowds at arrival

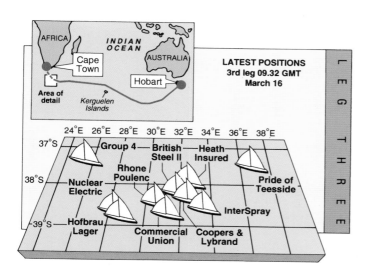

Nuclear Electric and Hofbräu Lager to fight over second place, 150 miles astern. There was little more than two miles separating these two but even fiercer was the battle for fourth place between Rhône-Poulenc, Commercial Union Assurance, Coopers & Lybrand and British Steel II, now within four miles of each other in terms of distance to sail to the finish.

So close was the tussle that the slightest change in wind transformed the order, as it did that day, making losers out of British Steel and CU. Tudor's crew dropped from fifth to seventh and Richard Merriweather's team, who had been chasing second place the week before, slipped another place back to fifth.

British Steel crewman Kevin Dufficy wrote of the frustrations: "Finally we have some pleasant conditions and celebrate with salmon fish cakes and jam doughnuts. Food plays a vital role in crew morale, especially if you have had the sort of day we have just had! Yacht racing is one of the most frustrating sports around. For the past 23 days we have been changing sails, often in appalling conditions, almost continuously 24 hours a day. We came from the back of the fleet up to second and then back to fifth. Locked in a really close struggle with three other yachts for days, we eventually got back to fourth, ten miles behind the second placed Rhône-Poulenc. In between were Hofbräu and Nuclear Electric three and four miles ahead. The crew felt really good, the hard work had kept us in the hunt. But a few hours later all that changed and we were back to seventh. Now we need more than fish cakes to get us going again!"

In stark contrast to the conditions they had faced across the Indian Ocean, the "Cape of Storms", as Good Hope is called locally, could provide little more than a whimper of wind to aid Group 4 Securitas round shortly after dawn on 18 May. Golding and his men then waited in vain for the breeze to fill in, banging the decks in frustration, as they took almost 12 hours to cover the final 30 miles.

"It's been a bad day, but a great leg," said the Berkshire fireman when Group 4 finally made it across the line. "The weather has been very different to the last leg across the Pacific. This time we were hit by a succession of very big storms, but we got into a good rhythm early on and the weather patterns became so regular we could almost plan our meals around them."

> "It's been a bad day, but a great leg."

Victory was sweet, but achieved at some cost to the boat and her crew. All 14 had been swept off their feet at some point during the voyage by green waves washing down the deck and, if they were lucky, had finished up against the catch-netting rigged up around the wheel. Some, such as Simon Littlejohn and Rob Coles, were less fortunate. Both were thrown up against the inner forestay while working on the foredeck and Littlejohn tore the ligaments in one knee. He had to have an operation on arrival at Cape Town which cost him his place on the yacht. Coles fractured his ribs and both were forced to spend

the last two-and-a-half weeks below decks working the galley.

It didn't help to hang on either, as Trevor Harvey proved. Instead of going with the flow and relying on a harness to arrest his progress over the stern, he kept a tight grip on the wheel when confronted by one wave. As a result the entire binnacle supporting the steering was bent back four inches by his weight!

Unlike the previous stage around Cape Horn, when six of the yachts suffered serious rig problems, the fleet had little visible damage to show for the ordeal. A small crack had appeared in the stainless steel decking around the starboard chain-plate on British Steel II, the yacht dismasted during stage two; Nuclear Electric had a nasty scar on her starboard bow after hitting an unknown object, and Pride of Teesside's cracked skeg led to a protest against the race organisers - later dismissed.

Chittenden's crew eventually finished third, three hours behind Hofbräu Lager and 24 hours behind Group 4 which cut "The Chittendales" overall lead to a tenuous 7 hour 56-minute margin over Golding's men.

"It was like the wildest rides at Alton Towers. The only difference was we couldn't get off," said Richard Rollinshaw, the baker on Nuclear Electric, once he had stepped safely ashore.

John Cox was also sorely tested. "By midway across I had had enough. Then they said there was yet another depression coming, I didn't think I would be able to take it."

Chittenden was more concerned by the lack of wind at the finish. After taking eight-and-a-half hours to cover the last 30 miles, he admitted: "We were all incredibly worried that this would be like our finish at Rio when we were becalmed for 11 hours just 200 yards from the finish line. We are just very pleased to still have an overall lead."

Pete Goss, in contrast, was elated by the performance of his Hofbräu crew now holding third place overall. "We have had survival conditions for a month and have only been racing for the past week. Now the Challenge is wide open. I can't wait to get started on the last leg back to England."

A day later they were followed first by Coopers & Lybrand, Rhône-Poulenc and then Heath Insured, leaving British Steel II, Commercial Union Assurance, InterSpray and Pride of Teesside to finish within eight hours the day after - another remarkably close testament to one-design yacht racing.

"Northward Bound"

Sailing Towards Reality

After the rigours of the Southern Ocean it inevitably took several days for Blyth's recruits to adjust to life's lighter side, even in the warm friendly, atmosphere of Cape Town. "I can't sleep for more than three hours without waking up to check the boat," complained Peter Phillips.

"If anyone offers you a trip round the world, ask which way they are going. If it is westward, say NO!" advised Kevin Dufficy, still white-faced after his ordeal through the southern seas. A glance at the bent and battered undersides of Teesside and Hofbräu Lager when they were slipped for repairs at the Royal Cape Town Yacht Club gave the best inkling of what these crews had endured. Both bows resembled the corrugated bonnet of a Citroen 2CV where the incessant slamming had hammered the 4mm steel plating as much as an inch out of shape.

One man certainly pleased to see land was Gary Hopkins, a paying passenger aboard Coopers & Lybrand who was seasick for much of the voyage. A building surveyor from Chigwell in Essex, he had planned to take on the entire challenge but, hit by the recession, had been able to make only half of the payments. Ironically, he took over the berth vacated at Hobart by British Steel employee Phil Jones. Like Jones, he spent much of the time strapped in his bunk, a slave to the bucket that was never far from his head, and wishing he was dead.

"It came as quite a surprise. I've sailed a lot, racing out of Burnham-on-Crouch, did all the Challenge training and never suffered from sickness" said the emaciated crewman once his feet had steadied on the Victoria and Alfred Dock. "Quite a few of our crew were seasick for three or four days out from Hobart but were able to bounce back. I had no problems until the seventh day when we were well into the gales and the boat began to pound," he recalled painfully.

Hopkins stood his watches until the constant sickness finally brought him to the point of collapse. He went down quickly and, sustained by little more than sips of water and the odd cracker, lost two stone during the ordeal.

What added insult to injury was the fact that he had paid good money for the experience and could not bear to take up his berth for the final so-called "fair weather" stage back to Southampton.

A few said they enjoyed it, including Pete Goss whose training as a Green Beret, one suspects, would have helped him

maintain those bright eyes and cheerful smile even if he had been a Christian facing Nero's lions. Another was Richard Tudor. "I definitely want to go back down there again. I've unfinished business to complete," said the British Steel II skipper with steely conviction.

But after a week of wine-tasting, tales of horror gave way to some of the humorous highlights. One was the rat said to be living aboard British Steel II. Marcus Gladwell, the fisherman from Southwold who had already hoodwinked his crew and onlookers with a display of shark fighting with a dead carcass found on the bottom of Wellington harbour, dreamed up the little fellow in an effort to improve morale on board during the last week at sea. "We had just dropped to seventh place and the mood was very low. Over dinner, I showed the opposite watch some 'droppings' I had made up from some of the freeze-dried food powder. They fell for it completely and Patrick Quinn ensured its success by saying that he thought he had seen one scuttle across the cabin two days before," Gladwell recalled. The second watch then spent much of their time off during the last week searching every nook and corner. "Giles Trollope even found its nest," Gladwell chuckled at the memory of his navigator uncovering a broken packet of custard powder. "God knows when they will realise it's a joke. They are still looking for it now. We might be able to keep this running all the way back to England."

Once the fishy tuna tale from Pride of Teesside had done the rounds, other incidents came to light. The crew from InterSpray provided the best example with a story that might also explain the bad luck that dogged them across from Hobart all the way back to Southampton.

Skipper Paul Jeffes is a racing man to the core, but not all his crew shared in his belief that fishing slowed the boat down. When Jeffes was laid up in his bunk with a badly poisoned leg soon after leaving Tasmania, other members of his crew slyly slipped the fishing line over the stern. To their eternal shame they caught not a fish, but an albatross after it had dived for the

Infolink Trophy winner for leg three, Mike Golding, the fireman from Berkshire and skipper of Group 4 Securitas

Tavern of the Seas: Cape Town, the most picturesque of the stopover ports, welcomed the British Steel Challenge crews with its customary warmth, and gave them a rousing farewell

lure and got its legs entangled in the line. "It was terrible. The bird was water-skiing behind the boat," one nameless crewman told us. "We tried jiggling the line to free it, and when that didn't work, reeled it in. The trouble then was that with a wing span of 6ft we had no hope of landing it. Then, just as we had it within a few feet of the stern, the boat was hit by a big gust and the line snapped."

The last Jeffes' crew saw of the bird, it was wallowing helplessly in their wake. Experts charitably suggested that its razor-sharp beak would take no time to cut through the line. The truth is InterSpray then faced every setback possible, falling into one calm after another all the way back to England.

Before leaving Cape Town, crews worked feverishly to divest their yachts of all unnecessary clobber. Both Nuclear Electric and Group 4 Securitas even went to the extreme of halving the number of oilskins to share among their 14 crew members. Chittenden's men, who took T-shirts and shorts as their only form of clothing, halved their supply of toothpaste and even threw off all their sea-boots, much to the delight of barefooted locals.

The Group 4 crew, now without Simon Littlejohn who flew home to recuperate after an operation to repair his knee ligaments, had one other card up their sleeve in the form of Vincent Geake, the former navigator from the British Whitbread maxi Rothmans. Geake is an acknowledged computer wizard with a keen interest in the world's weather patterns and had been working with Golding's team since before the race started, providing clues to probable weather patterns.

His fame spread to Teesside and, before the previous leg

commenced, Pride's sponsors decided to support Geake to fly to Sydney and analyse the weather in the Indian Ocean for their own yacht. But when Geake's findings became available, skipper Ian MacGillivray, ever the Corinthian, would have none of it. In his view, such privileged information given out after the fleet had left Southampton was outside assistance. But poison to one is invariably meat to another, and Golding welcomed Teesside's rejected advice with open arms. Was it pure fluke that Group 4 should win with a day to spare and Teesside should finish last? The next leg would perhaps provide the answer.

> "This is going to be a sprint to the finish and we are basically starting on level terms."

As crews began to prepare for restart, race leader John Chittenden had two things on his mind - Group 4 Securitas and Hofbräu Lager. Golding's men had narrowed Nuclear Electric's lead down to seven hours 56 minutes and Goss and his crew were hovering in third place a further 11 hours astern. "It's going to be a severe tactical test. It is always difficult to cover two boats at once, especially if they split away from each other," predicted the Nuclear Electric skipper.

Goss promised to give his rivals a good run for their money. "I'm not concerned about our deficit. Nineteen hours is nothing if they get caught in the Doldrums or Azores high-pressure system. This is going to be a sprint to the finish and we

are basically starting on level terms."

One of the best features about this race was that all ten yachts were equal in every respect. That gave each crew an equal chance of being first back to Southampton, whatever may have befallen them before.

The team with perhaps the strongest desire to steal the limelight was Richard Tudor and his crew. After winning the first stage to Rio, their dismasting midway across the Pacific had left them with no chance of winning and now they were almost 12 days behind the leaders. "The crew are really fired up. We've all got something to prove to ourselves as much as to everyone else. We are going for it from the moment the gun fires," said Tudor.

As dawn broke on Saturday 15 April, the fleet was greeted by massive 25ft swells that knocked the wind, if not the stuffing, out of some crews as they readied themselves in Table Bay for the midday start of this final 6,400-mile stage back to Southampton. Chittenden's crew were certainly caught unawares by the towering seas and found themselves starting five minutes behind the fleet after having the breeze shaken out of their sails.

The seas caused further confusion when the first turning buoy, laid in the centre of Table Bay, was swept out of position. "By the time we had spotted it and I had gone below to check its position, the buoy had drifted more than a mile," said Teesside's Ian MacGillivray. He was not alone to complain, for both Heath

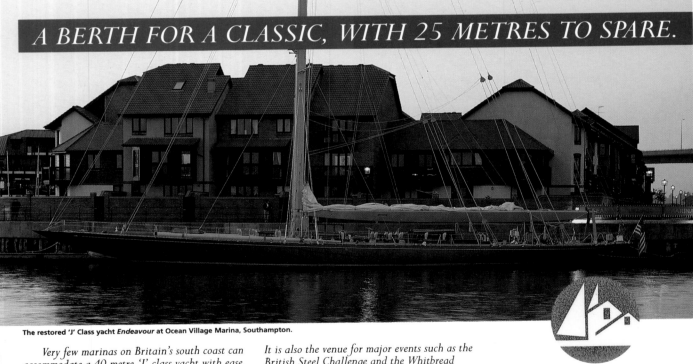

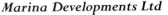

Insured and InterSpray were forced to gybe round for the mark and left the Bay with red protest flags fluttering in their rigging.

Other crews had no difficulty in locating the mark however, and the eagle eyes on British Steel II helped Tudor and his crew gain the early lead, a short distance ahead of Commercial Union Assurance.

The confusion also helped Chittenden to redeem himself. Within a day he had Nuclear Electric fighting for the lead once more a mile behind Group 4 Securitas after British Steel II, Interspray and Hofbräu fell into calms closer to the coast.

Overnight, the spectre of that albatross took no time to rise up and haunt the InterSpray crew once more. Julian Wells, the vet on board, reported on their latest bad luck: "During the night, the spinnaker pole topping lift eye broke away from the pole and resulted in the heel flying up and out of the track. Only prompt action to drop the spinnaker prevented further damage and all is in normal working order again." As an aside, he also reported: "Ruth Colenso, our new one-legger, is finding her sealegs now after the first day chop reduced her to bucket watching."

Running under spinnakers through the South East Trades, the yachts soon picked up their skirts and were tracking northwards at high speed as Nuclear Electric and Group 4 traded the lead between them. The picture only changed after five days at sea when British Steel II suddenly stormed through the fleet when the early leaders became ensnared in the south Atlantic high pressure system. Tudor and his crew, who had nothing to lose from taking a flyer away from the fleet, had been setting a solitary course well to the east of the other yachts since the start. Unaffected by the easterly-moving high pressure system, they moved from last to first.

Richard Merriweather and his crew on Commercial Union, who had been challenging Group 4 and Nuclear Electric for the lead, were quick to take a cue from British Steel's spurt and, after gybing eastward, held second place. For the others fighting a private duel for overall honours, the drop back was almost as dramatic. Both Group 4 and Nuclear Electric were by now struggling to better six knots, three knots less than the two pace setters who had built up a 30-mile lead on the fleet.

Reporting from British Steel II, a buoyant Kevin Dufficy reported: "There is everything to play for. For every yacht the

Bowling homeward: Commercial Union sets her kite. "We've had more spinnaker peels than hot dinners," says Sue Tight, as the crew traded top billing with British Steel II

chance to be first into Southampton; for most crews the chance to win the race overall; for every crew volunteer the opportunity to say - 'I did it. I sailed round the world.'"

Two days later the smile was wiped off his face when the British Steel crew spotted Commercial Union on the horizon, gybing across six miles ahead of them to become the seventh leader within a week. Now it was Sue Tight's turn to be pleased. "We've had more spinnaker peels than hot dinners. Foredeck crew are getting pretty slick at responding to sail changes and determined to keep our spinnakers in one piece. They have a few more miles to cover! We expected SE winds so gybed inshore to pick them up. Instead we got SWS winds which have allowed us to sail at 10 knots right on course. Magnificent sailing......"

Seventy-five miles to the south things were a little more frenetic. "It has been an amazing 24 hours," reflected Greta Thomas the latest recruit to Nuclear Electric. "After 600 miles we have our two main rivals in sight. We are wondering if this incredibly close racing will continue for days or weeks. It's certainly a great way to improve our sail trim. Under this king of pressure, we are constantly tweaking, questioning and trimming."

Over on Pride of Teesside, now riding in ninth place, MacGillivray's crew were given a short-term shock when they thought they had run into an oil slick. The skipper reported:

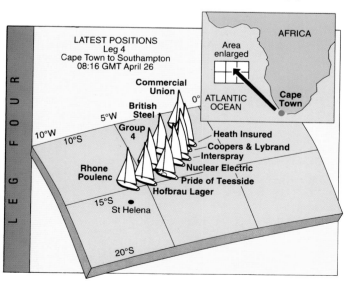

"The foredeck was covered with black streaks. Gary Bailey collected some multi-purpose cleaner from the galley to start the awesome task of cleaning up only to find that the black substance dissolved in water. On closer inspection, it turned out to be a form of plankton of such density that it appeared to the eye as oil. What caused it to gather so thickly I have no idea."

The trade winds continued to provide the fleet with thrilling spinnaker ride towards the Equator. Commercial Union reported a top surfing speed of 17.1 knots at one point on 23 April. Merriweather praised his crew for the constant sail trimming that had helped them to cover 1,000 miles during the past five days. Rob Haine, the British Steel II crewman who lost the tip of his thumb during the first stage of the race, was just as ecstatic. "The sun is warm enough for T-shirt and shorts and much of our off-watch is spent on deck - something that was unthinkable during the past 15,000 miles through the Southern Ocean."

> "We are wondering if this incredibly close racing will continue for days or weeks."

Two days later, British Steel II had stolen a two-mile march on Merriweather's crew, the eighth such change of leadership in as many days as the fleet pressed northwards in a wide arc fanning out eastward of St Helena. The one surprise was the poor placing of Nuclear Electric which had dropped to eighth. Chittenden suspected weed around the yacht's propeller and, after consulting Race HQ, started the engine up and put it into reverse. That brought the boat to a halt and cost the crew three miles over their nearest rivals - an expensive diversion in racing this tight.

These weed problems, coupled with a shift in the wind, allowed Golding and his crew to break clear of the Chittendales'

Sailor Bill's final voyage: the tragedy of Bill Vincent's loss on 29 April marred Heath Insured's homeward run

cover and claw eastward to close the gap on the leaders. By the end of the day the advantage had grown to 37 miles, the equivalent of four hours' sailing - half Nuclear Electric's overall lead.

With the fleet fanned out over a 120-mile radius, the relative distances to the finish became confusing. BT's satellite-tracking system measured the yachts against a preset Great Circle course and any that strayed from it invariably fell down the official leader board. That may well have been the case with Commercial Union that day. Though falling two miles behind British Steel, Merriweather's crew were more than 60 miles

north as Tudor and his team began to make a run to the west. Both yachts, however, enjoyed a 50-mile lead over a second group fighting for third place. Vivien Cherry's Coopers & Lybrand, which had held this position for much of the week, suddenly slipped back. It transpired that a stomach bug had spread through her crew, taking the edge of their performance. They now faced a three-pronged attack from Group 4, 260 miles to their west, Heath Insured, 30 miles to port and InterSpray which by then was so close that the two crews could eyeball each other.

On board Heath Insured, "Radio" Rayson was at his most radiant. "Nature does not let us down. Golden sunsets form behind blueing clouds over a purple sea. The nights are now balmy and the days crisp. Crew morale is high, the boat slips along at 10 knots without the effort of the Southern Ocean to make her go. Below, life is on the level and memories of falling from bunks fade. In the galley, Carol Randall, injured leg braced from ankle to upper thigh, performs miracles. Fresh this, fresh that, eggs and bacon for breakfast, curried coleslaw for lunch. 'Is this really Heath Insured?' asks one crew gastronomically bemused. The rest look nervously for signs of Carol's recovery, winch handles at hand..."

A day later, on 26 April, this game of musical chairs showed no sign of stopping. Nuclear Electric pulled back three places overnight and reduced Group 4's hard won advantage to 19 miles as Golding's crew sat on deck hand-stitching the leech and foot tapes back into their heavy weather spinnaker. Chittenden, however, was more concerned with the next hurdle - the Doldrums. "That's where the next phase of this race will be won and lost," he told his crew. "The current loss of 18 miles to Group 4 is of no consequence compared to what could happen in the calms just across the Equator. We could see changes of 120 miles there," he warned them.

Kevin Dufficy had other things on his mind. "I dream that as we approach Ocean Village, Southampton, the quayside is packed with bank managers, VAT inspectors and various debt collectors. They may not be sympathetic to the claim that whilst I haven't earned any money, I have discovered myself. 'Self awareness and self fulfilment do not balance the books' - I hear them saying."

The memory is a strange thing. Having spent three months in the Southern Ocean and been terrified, I had crossed sailing off my wish-list. Suddenly, on our way up the coast of Africa, it is all sunshine and spinnakers; sunbathing and surfing. Perhaps when we approach the finish we should just keep on going - especially if those bank managers are standing there!"

As the fleet drew closer to the Equator and latecomers had begun to quake at the thought of what fate would befall them at the hands of King Neptune, humour raised its head within the fleet when the voice of Captain Spencer Drummond was picked up on the radio moments before the inter-yacht chat-show commenced. Announcing a hazard to shipping in the form of countless semi-submerged containers floating east of Madeira, he ordered the fleet to pass west of the island. The mimicry certainly fooled Richard Tudor who solemnly told the fleet the following day that he had been in touch with Race HQ and that the good captain had made no such broadcast.

Inset: hand-stands for joy aboard Pride of Teesside as she crosses the Equator once again, back into the Northern Hemisphere

Halyard riding was one exhilarating method of keeping cool in the heat of the battle

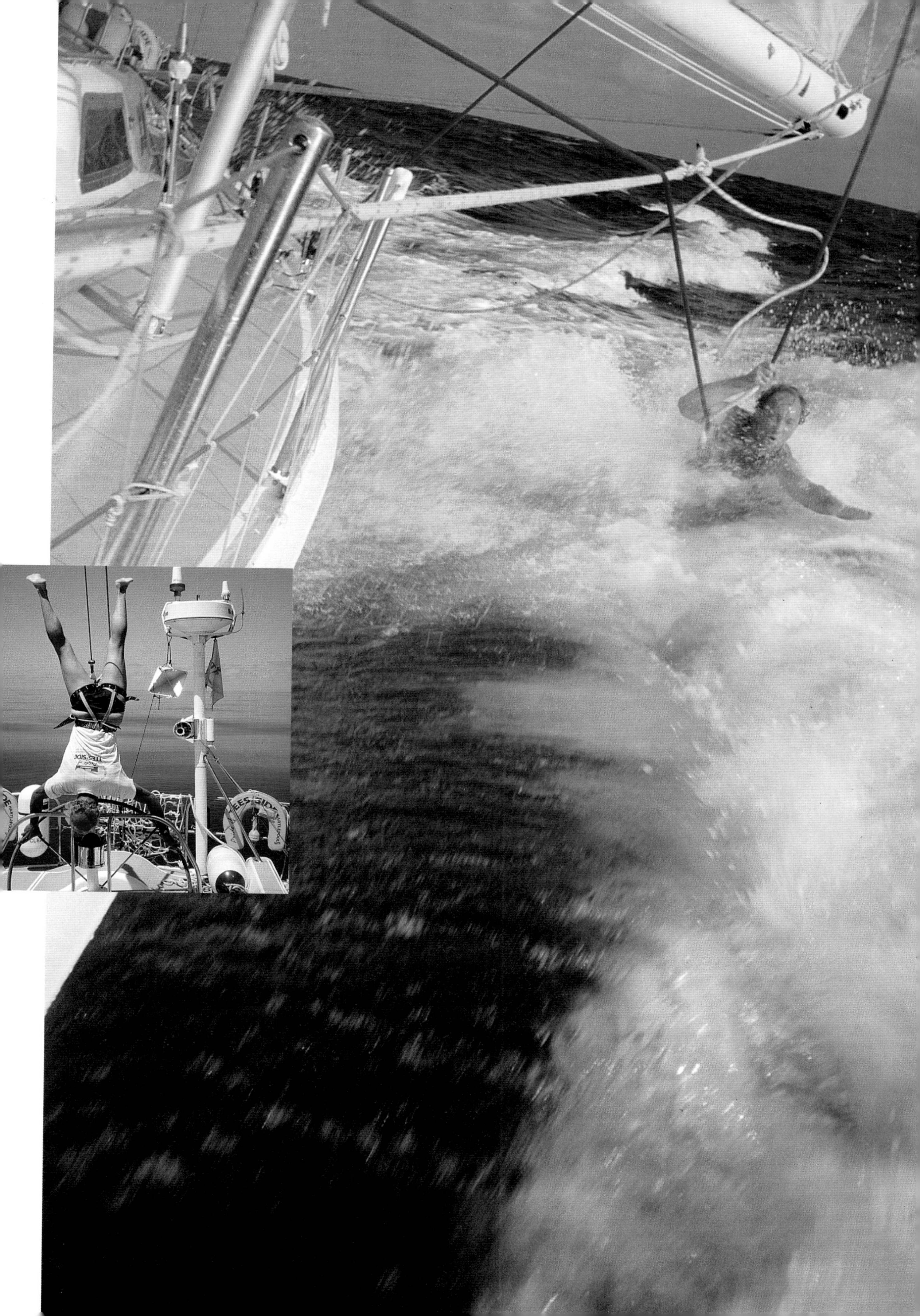

But the smiles and winks this prank generated were washed overside with the tragic news late on 29 April that Bill Vincent had been lost overboard from Heath Insured. The 47-year-old carpenter from Bath had inexplicably dived off the stern of his yacht into the warm seas of the Atlantic at 03 05 S, 07 56 W and was never seen again.

Adrian Rayson, who was steering at the time, told the official enquiry called at the end off the race to investigate his death, that Vincent, who was wearing only swimming trunks, eased the spinnaker guy on a cockpit winch then stepped up on the aft pulpit and dived overboard. "It was a perfectly executed dive" he told the Department of Transport official.

Skipper Adrian Donovan was up on deck within 12 seconds and had put the man-overboard routine, which they had all practised so thoroughly before the race, into action within half a minute. What followed was, in the words of Alan Green, Race Director of the Royal Ocean Racing Club, a copybook search that lasted for 18 hours until medical experts advised that he could not have survived. "We searched the area for two hours until dark, then continued with a spotlight," Donovan reported at the time. "Conditions were southwesterly force three to four with a moderate swell and a few white horses. We put two crew, Samantha Brewster and Dave Spratley, up the mast to the second spreaders. We also had lookouts in the pulpit, port and starboard sides of the boat and on both quarters."

The problem for the crew was that, while Vincent's exact position was known from the yacht's GPS satellite navigation system and they recovered dan-buoy markers and horse-shoe life rings thrown overboard moments after he left the yacht, he was not seen again after turning round briefly to look at the yacht while swimming away from her stern.

No one will know the extent of the mental turmoil that led him to take his life, but this self-confessed tearaway who had spent half his existence in reform schools and institutions before abandoning a life of petty crime when he met his wife Pauline 20 years before, will be remembered as one of the great characters of the race. He had been one of the first to sign up for the Challenge and, undaunted by the £15,000 or fact that he had never sailed before, underwent two years of intensive training before the start.

To help pay the costs, his school teacher wife took on a second job and their two children contributed from their paper-rounds and odd jobs.

During the Rio stop-over, it was Bill who sought out Ronnie Biggs, the fugitive Great Train robber, and introduced him to other crews in the race. "I've given up crime - I could never make it pay," he had joked to the escaped celebrity. The two were kindred spirits and struck up a strong bond

during the month-long stay. Indeed, it was Biggs who came to Vincent's aid one night when he was mugged in the city.

The reformation of the man, who became the fleet's official barber, came late in life. He told the author in Rio that his wife had been the steadying influence. "She put me on the straight and narrow and I've not looked back since I met her."

But if his marriage was one turning point, the Challenge was another. Right up until Cape Town, he typified the gritty spirit that brought these amateurs through the worst of the southern seas. Perhaps he just could not come to terms with the fact that the excitement had to end sometime.

The enquiry concluded that Vincent had been lost at sea, believed drowned, and the chairman went out of his way to praise the actions of both the crew and race organisers. But to most of us who got to know Bill well, it seemed such a waste that the Challenge that had given him such a wide outlook on life should also consume him.

Hofbräu Lager's crew celebrate crossing the line
Below left: Action aboard British Steel II which very nearly stole a march on the fleet.

Both Nuclear Electric and Interspray crew turned to aid in the search, but being at least 10 hours away, the Challenge HQ released them to continue the race once it was realised they could provide no practical help.

All ten yachts crossed the Equator on 2 May spread out over a 500-mile band and began the game of picking their way through the fickle winds, thunderstorms and oppressive heat that make up the Doldrums. The changing winds gave an initial advantage to Group 4 Securitas which moved two miles closer to Southampton than Commercial Union. However, with just 35 miles dividing first from fifth (Rhône-Poulenc), the race remained wide open.

Two days later all were within the grip of this humid hothouse where a roulette wheel would be a fairer way to judge the winner. Fortune smiled on Commercial Union making an extreme eastward run through the Doldrums, for despite blowing out a spinnaker, Merriweather and his crew opened up a 22-mile lead over Chittenden's team.

There was no such encouragement for Peter Phillips whose yacht lay trapped in calms 350 miles to the west. The Rhône-Poulenc skipper reported: "All in all a terrible day. We have gone into the Doldrums and stopped while everyone else has closed up and wiped out all our gains. We hardly moved all day, and in one period of seven hours, covered only 12 miles, while others behind have gained as much as 30 miles. Our strategy is right because the Doldrums are widest near the land and narrowest to the west of us. Trouble is, it is now a lottery, for no two boats have the same wind. Only time will tell over the next couple of days which of is in the best position," he said after slipping a place to sixth."

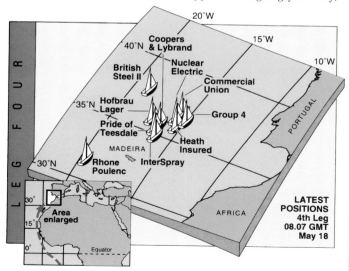

> "Trouble is, it is now a lottery, for no two boats have the same wind."

By contrast, Pride of Teesside had more wind than MacGillivray's crew could cope with. "We were hit by a tropical thunderstorm. It came in so suddenly that we were caught with full main and genoa set with 50-knot winds that pushed the boat at 13-14 knots through completely flat water," Ian recalled at the finish. "It was an incredible sight and the boat generated a huge quarter wave as we struggled to claw down the genoa and set a reef in the mainsail."

The gust lasted well over an hour and sped Teesside past Rhône-Poulenc on the leader board.

Commercial Union had a similar experience. Crewman Jock Stevenson-Hamilton complained bitterly: "The wind just cannot make its mind up. Yvonne Taylor and Jim Kinnier-Wilson, our two meteorologists, have found us some wind to the east which has enabled us to make good progress on the fleet. At one point we were doing 10 knots in the right direction and had a school of dolphins piloting the boat. At other times though, it has just been boxing the compass."

Another to gain was InterSpray which moved up to eighth place at the expense of Hofbräu Lager, now following an extreme course on the westerly side of the fleet. Pete Goss admitted to some frustration. "Progress is a complete lottery. If a cloud envelopes the boat and happens to be going your way, then progress is made, but there is nothing one can do when there is no wind. This is like sitting in a dentist's waiting-room with an open appointment. One might waltz in and get away

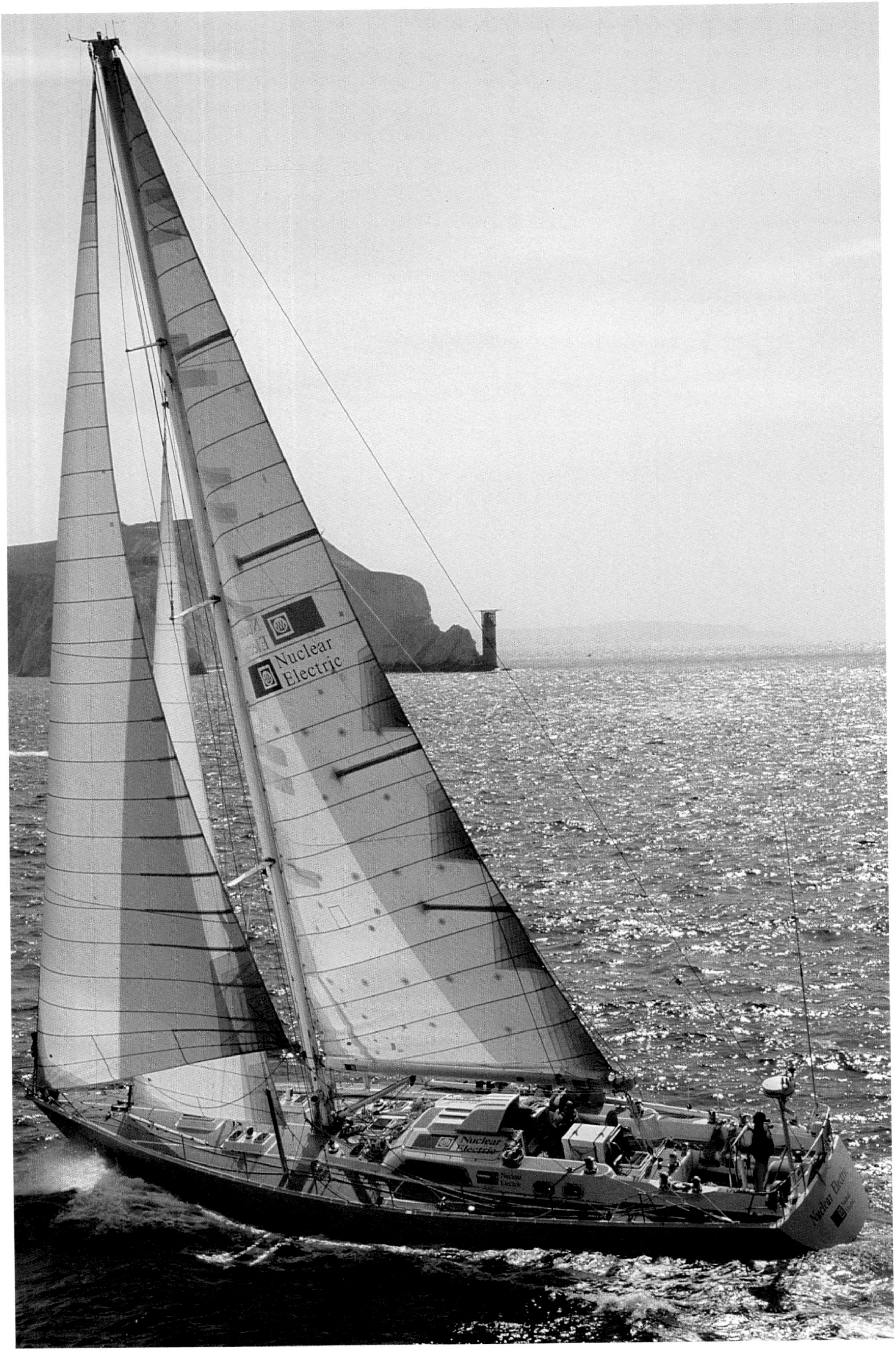
Nuclear
Electric
Nuclear
Electric
Nuclear
Electric
Nuclear Electric

Portrait of three winners: John Chittenden's winning Nuclear Electric, Group 4 Securitas and Hofbräu Lager were consistently sailed throughout the 28,000 miles. Any one of them could have won. Had not Mike Golding and Group 4's crew diverted to Florianopolis to repair their forestay, they might well have clinched victory. Pete Goss on Hofbräu was similarly unlucky to have become becalmed so long in the Doldrums

Surrounded by a small armada, Nuclear Electric and her crew slip back up the Solent, to the finish at Southampton. The outcome lay in the balance right to the end

with a check-up, or endure hours of painful treatment."

The big break finally came with a whoosh on the evening of 5 May. Mike Golding reported it thus: "We were shocked into life by a 45-knot squall. Caught with full main and genoa set, Group 4 laid right over on her side with sails flogging. The foredeck crew, who were part-way through changing to a smaller sail, battled to get both sails down in torrential rain. After 40 minutes we were at full speed again with the third reef in the mainsail and storm sail set."

As the North East Trades began to bite, and the fleet began to tack up the African coast, sightings became more frequent. According to BT's satellite tracking system, Group 4 and Commercial Union shared the lead, and Sue Tight reported spotting another yacht on CU's port bow. Even more extraordinary, Tudor's crew was forced to dip under the stern of Nuclear Electric when Chittenden, who had the right of way, boldly called "Starboard!" on them.

All told it was a remarkable 24 hours for Golding and his men. The previous day they had lost four hours going to the aid of a fishing boat that had broken down eight days before. "There were 15 Africans of all ages on deck looking decidedly worse for wear," he reported when alerting the rescue authorities at Falmouth. The Group 4 crew passed across what food they had to spare and left the bedraggled fishermen still at anchor after reassuring them that help would be on its way.

Golding and his crew were in their rights to claim this lost time at the finish which must have concerned Nuclear Electric's

men. Colleagues of Michael Calvin, the Daily Telegraph man on board, began to wonder if he was leading them on a pub crawl through the islands.

The tension generated by such a close-fought race finally erupted into a political storm over a ruling issued by Race HQ on 11 May which appeared to allow sponsors to send their yachts weather information and regular updates on the positions of close rivals. One crew complained that other teams were getting private information.

"What it does is substantially change the rules two weeks before the finish," one skipper complained as John Chittenden's Nuclear Electric edged ahead of Commercial Union and closed to within 23 miles of Mike Golding's Group 4 Securitas, his leading rival for overall honours.

"We are now sailing downwind with the spinnaker up and it is a hair-raising ride."

The arguments began with a message sent by Captain Spencer Drummond, the race secretary, to all yachts, confirming that sponsors could send information that was publicly available. Most, if not all, skippers had believed this to be outside assistance, and during a heated inter-yacht chat show, they decided to disagree with the ruling. However, as one crewman put it: "The fact that the ruling has not been withdrawn, must make some crews feel as if they should get their sponsors to gather as much weather information

Ocean Village: the welcome at Southampton was spectacular as eight yachts arrived on the same day, leaving just Interspray and Heath Insured to bring up the rear, though not in the overall standings, some days later

crew trailing two hours astern.

By 9 May this lead had extended to 49 miles as the fleet led by Group 4, a handy 70 miles to windward of second placed Commercial Union, tacked away from the African coast in the hope of picking up stronger winds offshore. Four hundred miles to their west, Pete Goss and his crew on Hofbräu Lager were headed on a solitary course towards the Cape Verde Islands, in search of a better wind angle to bring them back on level terms with the leaders. The tactic had yet to pay any dividends, for Hofbräu was then trailing ninth, 260 miles behind Golding's

as possible, simply because their opponents may be doing the same."

Another crewman called the decision "a shambles and act of incompetence. Outside assistance in whatever form is outside assistance and it has always been accepted that this is not allowed" he complained.

The problem for the race organisers was that it was almost impossible to monitor or stop supporters sending privileged information to the yachts. The six-hourly position updates provided on BT's fax database, for instance, gave details of the exact course and speed of each yacht, which was invaluable information to a close rival sailing just over the horizon on the opposite tack.

The race organisers moved quickly to overcome that by sending the information to all the yachts the moment it was published on the BT system, but they appeared powerless to stop supporters from sending vital routeing information.

All this was forgotten on 16 May when a south-westerly gale suddenly hit the fleet as the leaders closed to within 1,500 miles of Southampton. Commercial Union Assurance benefited most. The overnight blast propelled them from fifth to first. British Steel II, 60 miles north of CU but 240 miles further out in the Atlantic sailing a longer course, also gained. Her fifth place was deceiving. Tudor and his navigator Giles Trollope had positioned their yacht to gain most from these strong running winds, while those to the east continued to experience lighter conditions.

Kevin Dufficy reported: "If anyone thought this round the world challenge was not a serious yacht race, they should have been in the North Atlantic last night. After enduring several days of light winds, a cold front came through to give us winds up to 43 knots. We are now sailing downwind with the spinnaker up and it is a hair-raising ride."

"We have averaged more than ten knots during the past eight hours and put the pressure on our competitors to sail even harder. Whatever the result, we will have been tried to the limit of our ability."

Tudor was banking on these winds veering round to the north west to strengthen British Steel's position and bring him within range of the top three, Commercial Union, Group 4 and Nuclear Electric, who were all now running directly north, less than nine miles apart in terms of distance to the finish.

But if the closeness of this finale was remarkable, the report from Greta Thomas on Nuclear Electric that day was extraordinary. "After more than 4,000 miles and a month at sea since leaving Cape Town, we have had our main rival, Group 4 Securitas, off our stern all day! It is certainly proving a test of nerve out here and focused minds intently on sailing as fast as possible."

For Chittenden it was all proving too much. Now out of tobacco, he had taken to rolling up the contents of tea-bags in the torn pages of discarded novels and smoking that to calm his nerves. Golding too was at the point of becoming a chain smoker.

Five hundred miles closer to the finish, and the situation was just as tight. As the fleet passed the Straits of Gibraltar, on 18 May, Commercial Union held a tenuous 11-mile lead over Golding's men with Chittenden clinging on a further 12 miles astern. "The pressure is beginning to tell," wailed Greta Thomas. "Talk about intense - the pressure on the skipper and crew is immense. There will be 14 very exhilarated but exhausted people on Nuclear Electric when we eventually set foot on dry land. It is like a cat-and-mouse game out here. One day we gain, the next, our rival does. But the gains are so small that it appears that the race for overall victory will continue right to the end."

And she was right!

Back in sixth place, Vivien Cherry reported to The Times: "The winds seem more consistent now with the long-range forecast showing a depression developing to give us a westerly gale up the Channel for what should be a match-racing finish. Every mile gained in the right direction over the other yachts is jealously guarded. We are working very hard on trimming for speed as we are now two sails down with our genoa and promotional spinnaker both ripped beyond repair."

It carried on this way right up the Portuguese coast, across the Bay of Biscay and into the Channel as all eyes turned to the track of British Steel II sweeping from the west towards Ushant. Would their gamble pay?

Rob Haine reported: "The atmosphere on board is fraught. With 360 miles to the finish we are averaging more than 11 knots and determined to catch the boats ahead of us. With 30-35 knots of wind behind us, and a following sea giving us the occasional surf at over 15 knots, we are careering along directly towards the Needles."

The outcome could so easily have gone any of three ways. Even when Group 4 swept up Southampton Water early on 23 May to claim victory on this final stage, Chittenden's crew were still battling in light airs against a foul tide to round St Albans Head on the Dorset coast with a deadline of seven hours 56 minutes to complete the final 40 miles. They made it with two hours to spare, but Chittenden had to admit it was close as his delighted crew fired champagne at each other on arrival at Ocean Village. "We were in sight of Group 4 on several occasions during the voyage and only lost ground on them during the last few days. At the end we were fighting an ebb-tide up the Solent and any slackening in the wind would have cost us the race."

It was the closest finish by far in any global marathon and capped a remarkable voyage undertaken by these ten amateur crews against the spin of the globe, many of whom had never thought of sailing before taking the gauntlet thrown down by Chay Blyth - and may never do so again.

Golding, was philosophical about his last-minute defeat. "It's been frustrating, but Nuclear Electric deserves to win. They have been consistent from the start. We could point to a few 'What ifs?' but so could everyone else."

But what if a broken bottle-screw, the first of six breakages to plague this fleet, had not cost his crew an unscheduled 48-hour stopover in Brazil? A shrug from Golding's shoulders said it all.

The Group 4 crew still had a great deal to celebrate. Not only were they the fastest yacht from Cape Horn to the finish,

GED

"As idle as a painted ship upon a painted ocean" (COLERIDGE)

Last but not least, Heath Insured celebrate their personal triumph

but had this final stage victory to add to their previous win from Hobart to Cape Town. They can also reflect on the fact that had they not lost those vital 48 hours diverting to Florianopolis, they would almost certainly have won overall.

Chittenden, who skippered the cruising maxi Creighton's Naturally in the last Whitbread Round the World race, thus became the first man to race around the world in both directions.

Among the thousands waiting on the quayside for the winning yachts was the former tennis star Christine Janes - born Christine Truman - whose eldest son Nigel had shocked the family by taking up the Challenge aboard Nuclear Electric. "Sitting watching the Nine O'Clock news with Mum and Dad is not going to be quite as riveting as sailing round the world," she observed, wondering what her son might do with his life now that the Challenge was over. "Having loved something very much myself, I knew what it was like to want to do something very much." What she had not understood was how much harder it is to watch and wait than to perform.

"Nine months have seemed like nine years. I'm far more nervous following it and now listening to it all than I ever was before a match. I have dark rings under my eyes. I could never have played in this condition. I'm very proud of what he has done, but I think it will be an awful letdown."

Hofbräu Lager, the pre-race betting favourite skippered by Pete Goss, completed the course third overall, after finishing at Southampton just nine minutes astern of fourth-placed Coopers & Lybrand - just reward for two years spent training these school teachers, dairy herdsman, market gardeners, steel workers and insurance salesmen for what was billed as "The toughest yacht race ever".

But even as the empty champagne bottles were being swept from the quayside at Ocean Village, Paul Jeffes and his crew on InterSpray were still paying the price for snagging their fateful albatross in the Southern Ocean. Indeed, Jeffes appeared ready to shoot himself after the yacht lay becalmed for more than a day almost within sight of the Needles. When he was warned that InterSpray just happened to be parked bang in the middle of a firing range, Jeffes told the authorities: "Frankly, a direct hit would come as a welcome relief, so carry on...!" They eventually finished well over a day after the leaders to take sixth place overall.

Donovan and his crew were last to return to Southampton. Their nine rival crews turned out in force to greet the dark blue yacht at the Needles and escort them back up the Solent. It was a remarkable show of solidarity, for most of Blyth's recruits took part in this spontaneous salute.

Although finishing last on this final stage from Cape Town, the Heath team ended the race seventh overall ahead of Rhône-Poulenc, Commercial Union and British Steel II whose crews also faced uphill struggles at various points during this 28,000-mile marathon.

And what of the romantic souls who hitched their fortunes to Blyth's star and who are now coping with the aftermath of that seductive call to arms by Britain's most charismatic yachting hero. Most of them sacrificed careers for the chance to follow in Blyth's wake. Families lost parents and bank balances were rifled. Many came back to face the reality of recession-hit

Britain. One crew member who works for British Steel returned to find his job had gone with the shutdown of the big Scottish Ravenscraig steel plant.

Rob Coles, the divorced printer aboard Group 4 Securitas, was typical. "The race has wiped me out financially. I've spent nearly £35,000, I've sold my house, my car and all I have left is a push-bike and a microwave."

"But money is not important. I know that if I can rebuild my life emotionally, I can sure as hell do it financially."

"What delights me about this race," Blyth had said before the race "is that it is about the determination and team work of the crew; most of whom knew little or nothing about sailing when they volunteered. It's thanks to people like them that we can demonstrate that excitement and adventure are not the sole property of the rich, elite or experienced." He was proved absolutely right.

"You couldn't put a price on the experience," said Nuclear Electric crew Nigel Janes. He would certainly agree with Mike Golding's words on arrival that: "It fulfilled everything I ever thought it would. Every single person among the crew believes the £15,000 was worth every penny."

All told, 179 recruits took part and 105 sailed round the world, leaving just five who fell by the wayside. John Cox, a crewman on board Nuclear Electric summed it all up at the finish saying: "It's been a fantastic experience, but thank god the world is as small as it is. I don't think I could have coped with more than 28,000 miles of it."

Peter Phillips, Rhône-Poulenc's ebullient skipper, had a final word to say of the crew he inherited and who served him so well. "They were a good bunch, but I can't imagine too many of them ringing me up in a few days for a beer. I've not been too friendly with them. I didn't see the need for it. I was paid by Chay Blyth to run the boat. For the crew it was a four-year adventure. The vast majority will probably never sail again. If they want to see wind and spray they'll probably go sit on a beach."

Perhaps the greatest achievement of the British Steel Challenge is that it has dispelled at a stroke the image of yachting as an elite sport. The absence of professional cynicism was refreshing. These were real people, with outside interests beyond the rarefied world of racing, not precocious rock stars. With calls to BT's fax progress reports totalling 110,000, it was clear that the public followed the race with a vicarious enthusiasm that only the Whitbread and the America's Cup can ever hope to rival.

Chay Blyth, who inspired so many to take up the gauntlet he threw down, now has plans for a second race in four years time taking the same general course around the world. "We want to make it an international event, attracting crews from other countries," he said. Already, his office has been flooded by inquires and some 400 names are now on the waiting list. In the meantime, the yachts will be taking part in several other challenges this summer, including the Cutty Sark Tall Ships race from Newcastle in July as well as cruises to the Arctic Circle and Fastnet Rock.

> "It's been a fantastic experience, but thank god the world is as small as it is. I don't think I could have coped with more than 28,000 miles of it."

Results of the Challenge

Leg Time – Total elapsed time from start of current leg to estimated/actual completion of current leg.
DDD HH MM SS – Leg time expressed in: Days, Hours, Minutes and Seconds.
* – Leg time modified by protest committee.

Arrival Times

Race Leg: 1 - Southampton to Rio de Janeiro

Yacht Name	Status	Arrival Time GMT	Leg Time DDD HH MM SS	Placing	
01: British Steel II	Finished	25 OCT 13:43:26	029 02 38 26	1st	
02: InterSpray	Finished	25 OCT 23:32:25	029 12 27 25	2nd	
03: Heath Insured	Finished	26 OCT 20:59:20	030 09 54 20	3rd	
04: Pride of Teesside	Finished	27 OCT 19:06:04	031 08 01 04	4th	
05: Hofbrau Lager	Finished	27 OCT 19:08:55	031 08 03 55	5th	
06: Group 4	Finished	27 OCT 19:07:03	031 08 32 03	6th	*
07: Nuclear Electric	Finished	28 OCT 08:45:26	031 21 40 26	7th	
08: Rhone Poulenc	Finished	28 OCT 08:57:03	031 21 52 03	8th	
09: Coopers & Lybrand	Finished	28 OCT 09:05:55	031 22 00 55	9th	
10: Commercial Union	Finished	03 NOV 04:58:45	037 19 53 45	10th	*

Additional Information:

The Protest Committee at Rio have penalised the following yachts for infringements at the start of the Race.
Group 4 by 30 minutes
Commercial Union Assurance by 2 hours.
Times given are corrected for these penalties.

Race Leg: 2 - Rio de Janeiro to Hobart

Yacht Name	Status	Arrival Time GMT	Leg Time DDD HH MM SS	Placing	
01: Nuclear Electric	Finished	03 JAN 14:26:03	048 22 26 03	1st	
02: Commercial Union	Finished	04 JAN 00:20:21	049 08 20 21	2nd	
03: Hofbrau Lager	Finished	05 JAN 02:29:55	050 10 29 55	3rd	
04: Coopers & Lybrand	Finished	05 JAN 08:43:19	050 16 43 19	4th	
05: Group 4	Finished	05 JAN 20:47:11	050 16 47 11	5th	*
06: Heath Insured	Finished	06 JAN 05:59:06	050 23 59 06	6th	*
07: Pride of Teesside	Finished	05 JAN 23:58:20	051 01 58 20	7th	*
08: InterSpray	Finished	06 JAN 20:44:30	052 04 44 30	8th	
09: Rhone Poulenc	Finished	09 JAN 22:58:40	055 06 58 40	9th	
10: British Steel II	Finished	16 JAN 06:15:00	061 14 15 00	10th	

Additional Information:

The Hobart Protest Committee have made the following decisions which are incorporated. Infringement at start; Heath Insured, 2 hour penalty. Redress; Heath Insured, 16 hours; Group 4, 12 hours and Pride of Teesside, 6 hours. British Steel II re-instated, her finish time being the time when she actually crossed the finish line.

Combined Times (Legs 1 to 2)

Yacht Name	Status	Combined Time DDD HH MM SS	Placing	
01: Nuclear Electric	Finished	080 20 06 29	1st	
02: Heath Insured	Finished	081 09 53 26	2nd	*
03: InterSpray	Finished	081 17 11 55	3rd	
04: Hofbrau Lager	Finished	081 18 33 50	4th	
05: Group 4	Finished	082 01 19 14	5th	*
06: Pride of Teesside	Finished	082 09 59 24	6th	*
07: Coopers & Lybrand	Finished	082 14 44 14	7th	
08: Commercial Union	Finished	087 04 14 06	8th	*
09: Rhone Poulenc	Finished	087 04 50 43	9th	
10: British Steel II	Finished	090 16 53 26	10th	

Additional Information:

The above final times now include all decisions of the Hobart Protest Committee. Yachts with a (*) alongside of them have a time adjustment, penalty and/or redress, from either or both Leg 1 or Leg 2.

Race Leg: **3 - Hobart to Cape Town**

Additional Information:

The arrival times have been confirmed by the Cape Town, Race Committee. The request for redress, from Pride of Teesside, was not allowed by the Cape Town, Protest Committee.

Yacht Name	Status	Arrival Time GMT	Leg Time DDD HH MM SS	Placing
01: Group 4	Finished	18 MAR 19:06:24	033 17 06 24	1st
02: Hofbrau Lager	Finished	19 MAR 12:54:58	034 10 54 58	2nd
03: Nuclear Electric	Finished	19 MAR 16:23:02	034 14 23 02	3rd
04: Coopers & Lybrand	Finished	20 MAR 19:06:58	035 17 06 58	4th
05: Rhone Poulenc	Finished	20 MAR 23:34:48	035 21 34 48	5th
06: Heath Insured	Finished	21 MAR 02:46:40	036 00 46 40	6th
07: British Steel II	Finished	21 MAR 12:48:09	036 10 48 09	7th
08: Commercial Union	Finished	21 MAR 18:44:40	036 16 44 40	8th
09: InterSpray	Finished	21 MAR 19:09:12	036 17 09 12	9th
10: Pride of Teesside	Finished	21 MAR 19:53:54	036 17 53 54	10th

Combined Times (Legs 1 to 3)

Additional Information:

The times are the totals of the 3 legs so far sailed. They include any penalty and/ or redress carried forward from legs 1 & 2. Yachts with such adjustments are marked with a (*).

Yacht Name	Status	Combined Time DDD HH MM SS	Placing	
01: Nuclear Electric	Finished	115 10 29 31	1st	
02: Group 4	Finished	115 18 25 38	2nd	*
03: Hofbrau Lager	Finished	116 05 28 48	3rd	
04: Heath Insured	Finished	117 10 40 06	4th	*
05: Coopers & Lybrand	Finished	118 07 51 12	5th	
06: InterSpray	Finished	118 10 21 07	6th	
07: Pride of Teesside	Finished	119 03 53 18	7th	*
08: Rhone Poulenc	Finished	123 02 25 31	8th	
09: Commercial Union	Finished	123 20 58 46	9th	*
10: British Steel II	Finished	127 03 41 35	10th	

Race Leg: **4 - Cape Town to Southampton**

Additional Information:

The Southampton Protest Committee noted that, in the event, yacht positions would not be affected by any claim for redress and that no yacht had made a claim for this reason. The provisional results for Leg 4 and the Race overall, i.e. Group 4 Securitas wins the Infolink Leg Trophy and Nuclear Electric wins the Challenge Trophy, are therefore confirmed.

Yacht Name	Status	Arrival Time GMT	Leg Time DDD HH MM SS	Placing
01: Group 4	Finished	23 MAY 06:33:58	035 19 33 58	1st
02: Commercial Union	Finished	23 MAY 07:27:27	035 20 27 27	2nd
03: British Steel II	Finished	23 MAY 07:43:32	035 20 43 32	3rd
04: Nuclear Electric	Finished	23 MAY 12:19:40	036 01 19 40	4th
05: Rhone Poulenc	Finished	23 MAY 12:41:51	036 01 41 51	5th
06: Coopers & Lybrand	Finished	23 MAY 21:08:44	036 10 08 44	6th
07: Hofbrau Lager	Finished	23 MAY 21:17:08	036 10 17 08	7th
08: Pride of Teesside	Finished	23 MAY 23:13:30	036 12 13 30	8th
09: InterSpray	Finished	25 MAY 14:48:03	038 03 48 03	9th
10: Heath Insured	Finished	27 MAY 10:49:12	039 23 49 12	10th

Final Race Results: Combined Times

Additional Information:

All combined times have now been confirmed by the Southampton Protest Committee. Nuclear Electric is the winner of the British Steel Challenge Trophy. Congratulations go to Skipper, John Chittenden, and all of his crew.

Yacht Name	Status	Combined Time DDD HH MM SS	Placing	
01: Nuclear Electric	Finished	151 11 49 11	1st	
02: Group 4	Finished	151 13 59 36	2nd	*
03: Hofbrau Lager	Finished	152 15 45 56	3rd	
04: Coopers & Lybrand	Finished	154 17 59 56	4th	
05: Pride of Teesside	Finished	155 16 06 48	5th	*
06: InterSpray	Finished	156 14 09 10	6th	
07: Heath Insured	Finished	157 10 29 18	7th	*
08: Rhone Poulenc	Finished	159 04 07 22	8th	
09: Commercial Union	Finished	159 17 26 13	9th	*
10: British Steel II	Finished	163 00 25 07	10th	

Race Communications

Race Management System developed by BT
in association with the Whitbread Round The World Race.

Reflections on a challenge of a lifetime

"The waves are awesome. They are 30ft high and we've had nearly 60 knots of wind across the deck. The biggest aim is to walk from one side of the boat to the other without a double somersault, the splits or a cracked bone."

Liz Macdonald, *administration officer on board Nuclear Electric*

"I'm not doing any more sailing unless I have a gin and tonic in my hand.
From now on there will be no more racing - just cruising."

Sue Tight, *management consultant on board Commercial Union.*

"Disney hasn't produced a ride that compares to the bucking, rolling motion and breakneck speed that 40 tons of steel can be subjected to by howling 60 knot winds and enormous seas."

Julian Wells, *veterinary surgeon on board InterSpray*

"The boat can't decide whether it's an aeroplane or a submarine. It's like driving your car as fast as possible over a humpback bridge and crash landing on the other side.
The are numerous occasions when all 40 tons of yacht and 14 souls inside are airborne."

David Willbank, *company director on board Pride of Teesside*

"They were a good bunch, but I can't imagine too many of them ringing me up in a few days for a beer.
When I went to Rio the yacht was in turmoil. I read the riot act and told them that there was no requirement I like them or vice versa. There was just one aim. To race the boat. That was what I was paid for."

Peter Phillips, *skipper of Rhône-Poulenc*

"Nature does not let us down. Golden sunsets from behind, blueing clouds over a purple sea.
The nights are now balmy and the days crisp."

Adrian Rayson, *company director on board Heath Insured*

"Our show-stopping stunt is the inverted wheel-spin - a very stylish manoeuvre, but one in which the landings still require practice. We have taken to naming the wave types. Along with the 'Bellyflop'
and 'Mountain', is the 'Galley Growler', the 'Bunk Bouncer', and after the 'Smoker Soaker' comes the 'Stern Whip'
and 'Corkscrew'. The 'Stern Whip' breaks over the stern quarter to give whoever is at the wheel
a real soaking. The ultimate, however, is the 'Corkscrew', since there is no warning - and no way out!"

Vivien Cherry, *skipper of Coopers & Lybrand*

"It was just one continuous round of changing sails in conditions that varied from flat calms to force 12 storms and wind-chill factors down to -30C."

Pete Goss, *skipper of Hofbräu Lager*

"I injected one side OK, but when I touched the other the needle must have hit a nerve because
he nearly shot through the cabin roof. I was more nervous than Rob and had to turn away to stop myself shaking."

Marcus Gladwell, *fisherman on board British Steel II*

"We are being washed, rinsed, spun, tumbled but definitely not dried. After a rogue wave filled our hot chocolate cups
with sea water and made the digestives go limp, we feel ready for our bunks. Nothing ever dries.
Dampness is a constant, unwelcome companion. All we can do is grin and bear it. But then, no one said it would be easy."

Simon Clarke, *company director on board Group 4*

"These boats are absolutely brilliant going to windward in strong winds."

John Chittenden, *skipper of Nuclear Electric*